Advance Praise for *When Magic Failed*

"I have never read a more enchanting account of disenchantment, just as I have never known a man more independently immersed in his culture than Fouad Ajami. *When Magic Failed* is an uncanny monument to both love and truth. Lucidly and lyrically, it dotes on the world that it leaves. This is a beautiful and honorable book."

—Leon Wieseltier

"In this powerfully written memoir, the late Fouad Ajami tells a story of profound disruption whose central theme is the impact of the modern world on the Shiʿite villagers of southern Lebanon. The narrative begins with a mother killing her daughter to shield her family from shame, and ends soon after a young man—the author—leaves Beirut to study political science in the United States. In between are a series of intimate portraits of men and women whose lives are variously destroyed, blighted, enlivened, or blessed by winds of change that can reach gale force. The characterization is acute, and the characters are unforgettable."

—Michael A. Cook

WHEN
MAGIC FAILED

A Memoir of a Lebanese Childhood,
Caught Between East and West

FOUAD AJAMI

BOMBARDIER
BOOKS

BOMBARDIER BOOKS
An Imprint of Post Hill Press
ISBN: 978-1-63758-175-9
ISBN (eBook): 978-1-63758-176-6

When Magic Failed:
A Memoir of a Lebanese Childhood, Caught Between East and West

Cover Design by Tiffani Shea

Beaufort Castle 1982 Courtesy of david55king, CC BY 2.0
<https://creativecommons.org/licenses/by/2.0>, via Wikimedia Commons.

All people, locations, events, and situations are portrayed to the best of the author's memory. While all of the events described are true, many names and identifying details have been changed to protect the privacy of the people involved.

Post Hill Press
New York • Nashville
posthillpress.com

Published in the United States of America
1 2 3 4 5 6 7 8 9 10

For Leila and Darius

Foreword by Peter Theroux

[handwritten annotation: current speaker]

It was in the mid-1990s that my editor at W.W. Norton contacted me to help clear the company's list of books under contract that it probably would never see. We agreed to cancel plans for a novel I had once promised, but that was long overdue, without any regret. In fact, this companywide clearing of the decks was a great relief to everyone involved, she confided to me, "Except in the case of a memoir we wanted from Fouad Ajami, about growing up Shiite in southern Lebanon."

I could sympathize. At the time I had never met Fouad, whom I admired greatly for his expertise on Middle Eastern literature and politics, and his beautiful prose, but our paths had not yet started crossing, except for a coincidence of shared interests. Fouad published his definitive *The Vanished Imam: Musa al Sadr and the Shia of Lebanon* the year before my little-noticed book, released only in London, *The Strange Disappearance of Imam Moussa Sadr* in 1987. I was both crushed and excited but dearly hoped he eventually would produce the memoir. In any case, two years later, in *Beirut: City of Regrets*, he sketched some details of the world of his youth:

*When we arrived in Beirut, it still had the feel of
a large town. There were sand dunes on Beirut's
southern approaches. And in the northeastern
sector of the city when we first moved into a
largely Armenian neighborhood, there were or-
ange orchards, a forest of pine trees, two or three
strawberry fields...[in] this squatter settlement
which the Armenians had built up....*

You had to look at this retro postcard of midcentury Lebanon
with nostalgia and amazement. Orange orchards and pine for-
ests in Beirut? And the muddy Armenian settlement he de-
scribed I knew four decades later as the dynamic suburb of Bourj
Hammoud, where Lebanese-Armenian friends always pressed
me to bring them "BH" car decals from Beverly Hills, on my next
visit from Los Angeles. Lebanon's ups and downs have made it
the most enthralling of time capsules, and Beirut itself has been
well documented.

Southern Lebanon—Fouad's ancestral home—was altogether
different. It was from that hinterland that the Ajami family would
make its journey to the cosmopolitan world of the city. Successive
erasures of Jabal Amil, from the Ottoman rule of Ahmad Pasha
al-Jazzar, who incinerated its written history in the late 18th
century, to Hizballah, which turned it to an armed camp—now
largely closed off to the world—had made that gambit urgent
but ever more challenging. We have had to wait for *When Magic
Failed* for a full account of this lost world.

After the tantalizing hints and fragments of autobiography
Fouad had shared in various previous writings, *When Magic
Failed* pulls back the veil on so much of what is unspoken. We
start *in medias res* with an honor killing—and not a mere sketch

but the deep story with all the personalities, competing societal stresses, muzzled dreams and contempt, the deed, and the aftermath.

Before being introduced to Beirut and the relatives striving against the odds in Saudi Arabia and West Africa, we find ourselves in a feudal and even medieval world where "women still dried and saved cow dung for fuel, where children used the bones of dead animals for toys," and where these women led laundry-laden donkeys past a Crusader fortress downhill to the "bristling rapids" of the river. Reader, have a look at Arnoun via Google Earth. These women steered their beasts down a 1,000-foot steep slope beside Beaufort Castle to the Litani River and back again, uphill to their chores, hardships, and husbands.

Fouad's mother Bahija, in particular had an uphill journey in life. She had married young to a *sayyid* from Jibshit, a harsh Jabal Amil village that would fall easily and early to Hizballah in the 1980s (the hometown of Sheikh Ragheb Harb, the "ayatollah of the suicides"). Abused and unhappy, she left that husband, and returned to Khiam the divorced mother of three, though without custody. Bahija then married Ali Ajami, and Fouad would be their second son. Ali would soon take up with a younger woman in nearby Nabatiyya.

It is Bahija whose character shaped not only Fouad but also his memoir. Her courage and spirit in the face of misfortune and constant humiliation seem to have imparted to Fouad his enduring passion for championing the underdog.

"I was and remained a discarded child of a discarded marriage," Fouad writes, but Bahija bravely used her leverage as the mother of sons with her father-in-law, Sheikh Muhammad, to preserve her dignity and that of her two sons. When Fouad

moved to Beirut for schooling at a rather dubious schoolhouse founded by his father, she followed.

Poor, unlettered, single, twice-divorced, this woman from the south of Lebanon had a survivalist mission in life that left her unintimidated by the Lebanese capital. Not that rural relatives did not cause embarrassment on their forays into glittering Beirut.

> We had older relatives—women with tattoos on their hands and their chins, women with head covers; men with red fezzes carrying baskets of figs and buckets of yogurt—who showed up right when the new city was about to be mastered, arriving unannounced to my remind [us] where we had come from. Abu Fawzi, the old great-uncle with the red fez and the red face, came to West Beirut with a live chicken as a present for his embarrassed nieces.

Fouad's generation was the bridge between the world of the ancestors and the modern post-war landscape of possibilities and change. Both gods demanded their tribute, but the political winds that were sweeping through the Third World transfixed the Lebanese youth. Fouad writes vividly of the wave of Gamal Abdel Nasser's popularity, during his teenage years. Nasser's politics, and the influence of the PLO when it moved from Jordan to Lebanon, sowed the early seeds of Lebanon's dark future, the narcotic of Arab nationalism that led to the 1967 military catastrophe, and Yasser Arafat's crew whose inner cadres would train the likes of Imad Mughniyeh, paving the way for the Iranian IRGC's virtual takeover of Lebanon. The pious Bahija, with a

villager's attachment to the land, was unimpressed by the great political questions:

"Two kinds of people you can never trust: The Communists because they don't believe in God and the Palestinians because they have no land," was her assessment.

The harshness of life for the southern Lebanese recalls the desperate life of southern Italy whose turf cultivated mafias and vendettas. Fouad writes that "[a] saying of hers from the old culture said, in effect, that one ought to kiss the hand one could not break and ask God to break it." This pan-Mediterranean sentiment would be echoed in Mario Puzo's *The Godfather*: "Kiss the hand you cannot bite and pray God to break it."

Fouad's adult life was that of a brilliant author, professor, and public intellectual, but we locate in his boyhood, and I suspect very much in his mother's influence, a humility and kindness that marked his entire life and work. He was the kindest and most unpretentious of men, and in this book, as in all his others, he tackles tragic and controversial subjects with immense insight and charity. This was unfortunately not the case with many of Fouad's detractors. Edward Said, in particular seems to have found Fouad's comparative authenticity maddening. Consider the paradox of Said being expelled from Alexandria's elite Victoria College in 1951 and sent to a tony prep school in Massachusetts—Northfield Mount Hermon School. Meanwhile, Fouad's reality, below the foothills of the actual Mount Hermon, was one of poverty and bloody Ashura rites. When Fouad underwent an agonizing village circumcision at the age of thirteen, Edward was an undergraduate at Princeton. "I desperately wanted to get out of the country," Fouad tells us candidly of Lebanon; of course, the USA would welcome the bright young Lebanese as a student and immigrant, and the embrace was mutual. Said, a US citizen from

birth, claimed exile from Palestine and used his elite Ivy League perch to preach against his father's adopted country.

Beyond Fouad's fundamental decency as a personal quality, it adds warmth and empathy to this book as it does to his others, as he has always written about Arab and Jew, Iranian and American, Kurd and Bosniac and Syrian and many more, with a profound respect for common humanity. I do not think he ever wrote a polemical sentence. Trying to think if I ever saw Fouad angry in print—I certainly never did in person—I can only think of his late chapters on women's rights and royal corruption in *Crosswinds: The Way of Saudi Arabia*, where his eloquent commentary becomes *pointed*.

This memoir contains precious details. We have the endearing village boy accustomed to haircuts from the local butcher, who discovered that in Beirut, real barbers did a thing called parting your hair—an innovation that made him feel like a million dollars. Like Naguib Mahfouz, he would discover America in movie theaters watching Westerns. In Nabatiyya, he and the neighborhood boys would watch High Noon's sheriff—underdog and loner—day after day, starting with "the thunderous applause that greeted MGM's lion." If Gary Cooper was Fouad's hero, William S. Hart was Mahfouz's, according to his story *The Cradle*. (Meanwhile, in Baghdad, young Sasson Somekh was enthralled by Betty Grable and Don Ameche in "Moon Over Miami," as recorded in *Baghdad, Yesterday*.) We see Fouad coming home empty-handed from his attempts to collect rent from ruined tenants, on behalf of his stern father ("a task I loathed"). But what sticks with us most is the heartbreaking life of the woman who raised the boy. Her spirit and her struggles infuse this memoir, as they did, no doubt, the sensibilities of the author.

Preface: An Act of Last Resort

When the mighty men came in from faraway places, they were strangers in their own homes. They were catered to, and they were kept in the dark. At some point fathers had to be brought in, implicated if you will, in the deeds of their sons and their daughters. But until that day dawned, until a daughter's transgressions became too public a matter to be ignored, or a son's ways could no longer be indulged, the men were pampered and kept ignorant. In the dark hours, when a reckoning could no longer be avoided, when the code of the place had been stretched to the breaking point, women had to do things of great cruelty. It was their burden, their task.

"She is the sister of men" was the highest compliment paid a woman who had to keep the world intact. To the women fell the task of smuggling diamonds from Sierra Leone because the skilled man of affairs who insisted that the high officials of the customs office were in his back pocket had gotten himself deported out of the country. The women were the ones who kept the constituents of a member of Parliament from finally having it out with him. They were the ones who prepared their sons for the duel and who stiffened their backs, reminded them of the hidden defects and the capricious ways of their fathers. And it

was their responsibility, of course, to keep the daughters in line. It was but a short distance from the daughter's conduct, it was implied and understood, to the mother herself. Better grieve for a daughter than play havoc with the order of things. This is the way things were discussed and understood here. And these were not merely words.

It happened among us that a woman of radiant strength had to "do something" about one of our daughters. The daughter's indiscretions had become too much to bear. The pompous and dangerous head of the household had signaled that his patience was running out. The sturdy woman would do the task that was hers to do.

Dalal was taken to her father's village for burial. The young woman, it was announced, had committed suicide. But it was known that her mother had struck. For some time, it had had about it an air of inevitability. Dalal had rejected all offers of help and punctured all the pretenses of her people's code. She had taken a step into a world she could not understand, and she had not known where to draw the line. The evasions and the consolations of the old world, the world of her mother and her aunts, were denied her. And the new ways were not yet internalized by the young woman who had just begun to see the world on the other side of the prohibitions.

Dalal had been given the best of what a generation on the make thought their children should be given. Parents who toiled in Africa made possible boarding schools, a new prosperity, a new kind of freedom, less encumbered and burdened ways of seeing and encountering things. The fears of the old world, the need to "walk by the wall" and to "kiss the hand that you cannot confront," the fear of the unknown and of the alien, the need to placate and to conceal—from all these, the young woman seemed

released. The limits that had defined the world of her mother and her aunts had irretrievably collapsed, and with their collapse it was hard to distinguish the permissible from the impermissible.

Dalal had ventured into the world on the other side of the divide; she was the first of her kin to venture beyond the line of familiar sounds and ways. She developed a sudden and total disdain for the ways of her elders, for their tales, for their dire warnings. They, in turn, were unable to explain how the young woman should juggle the two worlds on the margins of which she had been placed. There came a time when Dalal began to complain about the women from the village, grandmothers and great-aunts who came visiting and who stayed at her home. She complained about their tattoos, about their wrinkled and toothless faces, about their prayers, about the ablutions that preceded the prayers. Above all, she complained about the smell that clung to the old women: she believed that they came with a special smell. And so she complained when they approached her and when they wanted to kiss her and wish her a life of honor and rectitude in the home of a decent, God-fearing man. Yes, Dalal, if you go about doing what is asked of you, if you follow the straight path, if you remain untarnished, if your reputation remains unblemished, happiness will come your way, and you will go from the home of your father to the home of your husband, an honored woman in whose reputation and whose conduct your father and brothers can take pride. No other man, no rooster or marauder, could humble your family by having his way with you. No ill-wisher could point to you whenever men and women sought to devour the reputations of others.

A relative of Dalal had prided herself on the fact that she had been the first to detect early signs of trouble. The world here came in very small ways and expressions. Dalal, the unwashed relative

from the village noted, did not invite relatives and friends to join a meal in the manner that such invitations should be extended. Dalal would only offer a single invitation. And when the guest insisted that he or she had just eaten, she always took them at their word and left them to eye the food. In the protocol of the villagers you had to extend endless invitations and literally drag the guest to the table. Then you watched the guests who had "just eaten" stuff themselves with abandon. The sophisticated young woman who had broken with her world would not play the game.

Nor would she willingly join, it was noted in retrospect, her mother and her mother's friends and guests when she was called upon to do so. In those sessions, young women learned the ways of their elders and the ways of the world. Whenever she was forced to participate, Dalal was never fully there. She would not engage in the sonorous language and its clichés; she would not play along. When a visiting friend of her mother told her that she and her son Shawki would make an ideal couple, Dalal had no qualms about saying that Shawki was a buffoon, that she had no interest in him whatsoever, that she would not be traded over coffee between two women from a passé generation.

A strange kind of honesty made Dalal see the hypocrisies of her elders' world. She began to see their deeds with new eyes, and gradually she began to judge. And because she did, she made her elders self-conscious. In her presence, her tough mother and aunts would at times squirm, and animated discussions would often come to an end whenever she walked in. But Dalal knew many things that they thought had eluded her. She tired of hearing pieties that were broken in daily practice. She had seen through the way of her elders. A few years before the trouble began, when still a young girl, Dalal had been used as an alibi for so many indiscretions by the older women in her life. She recalled the

record of each of the virtuous women who later came to lecture her about her own behavior. She laughed at the pretensions of the cuckolded husbands who knew perfectly well what was going on but preferred to look the other way.

Dalal had seen her pretentious paternal uncle Abu Hassan pass himself off as a man of the world, proudly displaying his women, letting the word out that he had finally seduced the voluptuous Leila and beaten out the competition. She then set this to what she knew of Abu Hassan's wife. Fair-skinned and vain, sure of her beauty and surer of the prerogatives of her new money, Abu Hassan's wife exercised her options as well. Two or three young men were in the wings, and it was rumored that they were being kept and provided for by the lady herself. Abu Hassan, Dalal knew, was both a rooster and a cuckold. In his own code, of course, he was a hunter and victorious. And in the pronouncements of his wife, the lady was queen in her house, a virtuous woman, cleaner than the ways of the cynical city.

Dalal's angle of vision enabled her to see the whole thing. Thus, when the virtuous woman said that she had spotted Dalal coming out of one of the furnished apartments on Hamra Street, Dalal recited what she knew of the other woman's comings and goings. When given a chance to deny what she had been charged with, Dalal refused. She would not participate in the charade and the theater that was Lebanese honor.

Early marriage suggested itself as a remedy. A man, it was believed, could rein in this kind of passion. Dalal would have her own home, shoulder new responsibilities, and the storm would blow over. She could then begin to make discreet trips to the tailor and offer the excuses and the evasions of other women of honor and responsibility.

A smug official of her father's generation was the man recruited to cap the volcano. Dalal's mother insisted that the man was Dalal's own choice, that it was an affair of the heart. A respectable dowry was given the unlikely couple. That was what money made in Africa was supposed to do—schools for the boys, dowries for the daughters. All prayed that the young woman's story was over. The determined mother had pulled it off. Dalal had walked from the home of her father to the home of her husband.

But the hopes turned out to be short-lived. As the young woman explained it, surely she deserved something other than what she got. The man in her life was a man of reasonable distinction. He had studied on his own and risen in the bureaucracy. But like her parents, Ali was a squatter in Beirut. He had about him the kind of clumsiness that Dalal's generation was so fond to point out and so quick to see in a man's speech, in the kind of tie he wore, in the way he shook hands with another. Ali was doomed in the young woman's eyes. He spoke the Shia dialect of the south. His French was not refined enough. His pronunciation amused the young woman and her sisters and her friends, all of whom had learned French as it should have been learned. That mighty badge of distinction, the French "r," just would never trip off his tongue the way it should have.

This was a world of mimic men. A dominant culture from afar, its acquisition and its display, its words and its jokes, were what set people apart from one another, what gave some of them a claim to power and self-worth. French pronunciation gave away the origin of men and women, the "age" of money in a particular household. New money spoke French one way, old money quite another. Boys who learned it under the husk tree—or was it the oak tree?—as Ali proudly proclaimed to have done, had no

chance of passing themselves off as sophisticated men of a very demanding place.

For young Tolstoy, who grew up in another culture that borrowed the trappings and the language of France for its court and its gentry and salons, the world was divided into two principal categories: *comme il faut* people and *comme il ne* faut pas. Tolstoy's *comme il faut* consisted "first and foremost in having an excellent knowledge of the French tongue, especially pronunciation. Anyone who spoke French with a bad accent at once aroused my dislike. 'Why do you try to talk like us when you do not know how?' I mentally inquired with biting ironies." Dalal's husband was definitely *comme il ne faut pas*. He knew nothing of the ups and downs of the relationship between Jacques Charrier and Brigitte Bardot. He was not familiar with the songs of Charles Aznavour and Sacha Distel. He told what, for his wife and her companions, were dreadfully boring stories about his triumphs in the bureaucracy, how this or that political boss needed his help and his patronage, how he had clashed with the minister and how the cabinet member had backed down because of his own superior knowledge and judgment. And he endlessly recited the familiar tale of how he had come into Beirut a quarter-century ago, how he had studied by kerosene lamp, how he had been one of the very first Shia boys from his world to graduate from the Lebanese University, how vain city boys had taunted him about his village and his past, about the speech and twang of the countryside.

The man of position had achieved all he could have hoped to achieve. But none of it mattered to the irreverent young woman by his side. That kind of tale would have filled the heart of a woman a generation older than Dalal with great pride. A different woman—denied, or spared, the world that Dalal had seen—would

have viewed his triumph as hers and that of her kin. But this was not the kind of man to cut an acceptable figure in the mind of a young woman who had grown up on a diet of French novels and films, who was courted by young men who had nothing to do other than sharpen their skills for the hunt. The world was what it was: Those effeminate young men with shirts unbuttoned to their navels, those dandies with their gold chains, with their melodramatic and insinuating puffs on *Gitanes* cigarettes, with new cars purchased by fathers who tackled hell in remote places, were surely no match for the sturdy qualities of Ali, with his yellow socks and bad French.

A real man, the sober official reasoned, should not be compared to such flimsy material. But this flimsy material was the new world, the world to which his treasured young wife belonged. Ali could not take the chic young woman back to where he and her father had come from, to the village where women still dried and saved cow dung for fuel, where children used the bones of dead animals for toys, where the slaughtering of a chicken had been, until very recently, a rare kind of occasion. How was he to communicate his world, and its wound and its limits, to someone who had not known it? How was he to tell Dalal of his cruel and terrifying father who humiliated him at every turn, and of the schemes of his stepmother, and of the distance he had to cover, forever on the run, unable to take anything for granted or to believe that he had anything to fall back on. His family had thrown him into a mighty storm, and he had been denied even the possibility of a graceful, quiet failure.

As the young woman picked on the filet mignon that was delivered to her doorstep, he very much wanted to tell her, while knowing full well how much of a bore he would be, of the white bundle that used to come to him while he was away at school, of

the few scrawny potatoes in it, of the endless diet of lentils, of the few thin loaves of peasant bread. Child, Ali wanted to scream, and he often did, where have you been and what have you seen? Such terrors and needs you have been spared.

Ali's generation had ploughed and had sown. Dalal was the harvest. Ali's generation, the generation of Dalal's father, had never bothered to inquire as to the ends of such striving and such toil. With a hellish world to their backs, they had kept on the run. And now the journey had culminated in *signé* shirts and blouses, in spoiled daughters and sons, in endless trips to reputable tailors, in dining rooms whose décor was declared obsolete soon after they had been lavishly purchased and proudly displayed.

The net that entangled women older than Dalal had failed to entangle her. She was too far gone to submit and to accept. Hard as her husband and her mother would try to keep her within the bounds, the young woman had become brazenly independent. She put very little if any effort and time into covering her tracks. The furious beatings administered by her mother and her husband were to no avail. On the morning after, she would plunge into it again, and ill-wishers would report her latest escapades. She was seen going into and coming out of this or that building; she had succumbed to the blandishments of yet another dandy, who would of course proudly report his latest conquest. In the carefree city that outsiders loved so much for its freedom and *joie de vivre*, the men and women who lived there were suffocated and hemmed in by so many curious, watchful eyes. Even the trees had eyes here, wrote the sensitive novelist Hanan al-Shaykh.

The gossips had seen it coming. The coroner's and the police reports on the terrifying day were met with the usual derision. The verdict of suicide, it was said, was secured by the payment of a large bribe. An ivory tusk, an expensive one of which Dalal's family was proud, exchanged hands and now adorned the coroner's living room. The officials were men of this society, after all: they knew their world and what it drove men and women to do.

When Dalal's body was taken to her father's village, her father and her husband were on hand to receive the condolences of those willing to offer it for a presumed case of suicide. But the day belonged to her mother, the tower of strength, the victim and the killer, sure in her grief that she did what she did for the sake of her other daughters, of her sons, of her home. The mother wailed, disheveled her hair, tore at her own clothes. She lined up all of Dalal's shoes, all those elegant shoes that the young woman had bought with the new money, and she spoke to them, it was said, about the young woman who had departed at so tender an age. She wanted Dalal, her Dalal, back. The *signé* shoes and the primitive code of honor: this country played them side by side.

A new and intense piety overtook Dalal's mother after the deed was done. A few years younger than my own mother, more exposed to the ways of the modern world, she would from then on accompany my mother to the holy shrine of Zaynab, the daughter of Imam Ali, in Damascus. When unable to do so, she would give my mother money and food to give to the poor who gather around the shrine and to the keepers of the shrine. The "secret" was shared between the two women on one of those journeys to Damascus. My mother was of two minds. She abhorred the deed, but she respected the mighty woman, and she knew what pressures and expectations had led her to do what she had done. Dalal, my mother said in defense of the woman, was a "piece of

her mother's liver"; nothing could be more precious than one's own child. But for some time Dalal's mother had been walking on eggshells. Dalal's father, now a prosperous man, had become restless. There was a danger that he would go beyond the common indiscretions, that one day a clever young huntress would lure him away from his family. A fallen daughter would serve as a convincing pretext, and the honorable man would be released in his own eyes from a home that had disgraced him. Sadness and grief, my mother believed, were better than disgrace. Dalal's mother had done a terrible duty, and decency required that those quick with a judgment should hold their tongues. Love, even maternal love, was a luxury here. It was given when it could be afforded, when men and women were not up against the wall, when others were not busy clawing away at their reputations, threatening them with exposure and disgrace, leading them into ditches where even "pieces of their liver" had to be surgically removed.

After the deed was done, Dalal's mother was never as commanding as she was before, her face never quite as bright. She no longer sounded sure of herself. The tough woman who had survived hellish years in Africa, who had single-handedly built a fortune after her husband was deported out of Ghana, who had put aside enough money to aid her father and a pretentious brother who could never make ends meet, who was generous to the multitude of relatives and of stray men and women who walked to her door with a hard-luck story, was transformed overnight. The letters that I wrote for her to friends and relatives in Africa, which previously had to be read back to her over and over again and repeatedly corrected before they met with her approval, became perfunctory. She trusted the writing, she said, and there was no need to read them back. The tales she told in the letters to relatives and friends were no longer crisp and chatty. They had

about them a matter-of-fact quality. One letter she had drafted to the overbearing husband, who was always in and out of the country, reported that all was well in the family, that she would see to it that all was well. This letter, and this section in particular, was read to her over and over again at her request. She wanted some hidden meaning to be transmitted, some knife perhaps to jump out of the pages, some sense of the cataclysmic deed she had done—a reminder to the honorable man that it was she who had to keep the world intact, that he would never quite understand her sacrifice and her anguish.

But the lines penned down by the letter-writer fell short of what she wanted. Arabic, the language of innuendo and hidden meanings and intricate alleyways, failed Dalal's mother on that day. And with uncharacteristic sharpness, she told the attentive scribe that his style had failed him, that he should be sure to plan a future that excluded a writing career. Yet she wanted the young man to stick around. She could bear no solitude. More than that: the drafter of the letters had been a peer of Dalal's. The two of them had exchanged jibes and put-downs; they had tested one another about the latest fads, about books and movies. Dalal had insisted that the Arabic letters at which the young man excelled, which had brought him not only spending money but also access to the secrets of so many families here, gave him away as a product of the old culture, that the formal structure of the letters, the frequent invocation of Allah's name and blessing and praise, confirmed an old mentality.

Dalal and her friend who was good at Arabic letters had shared what they had shared. It was enough for Dalal's mother that the young man stuck around that day. They both knew when they were both speaking of the dead. They both knew the hidden language of lament and yearning. The mother very much wanted

her daughter's friend to know, without uttering a word about the entire matter, that it had all been a tragic act of last resort, that nothing else could have been done, that a mother's grief exceeds the imagination of the closest, the kindest, the most pious of friends.

I

I was born among a rural population at a time when the balance between man and the land was eroded. It was a time when men pledged eternal fidelity to the land and scrambled to find a way out of its harshness and incompleteness. The land was being annulled. What was there, at the time of my birth in 1945, in the southern, predominantly Muslim Shiite hinterland of Lebanon, was a people of sullen temperament who derived their ethos and their phobias from their land as they brooded about what the world held in store for them.

There were books and manuscripts, I was told, but they had been burned. In 1781, in retaliation for Shiite rebellions and disobedience, the Turkish Governor Ahmad Pasha al Jazzar—"the Butcher"—had the books taken to his capital in Acre on the backs of camels. These Shia books, books that would have told us of our history and our achievements, were said to have kept the ovens of Acre going for six days. He had been the terror of the land, this Ahmad the Butcher. A soldier of the Ottoman Empire born in

Bosnia, Ahmad Pasha had spread his dominion over the coastal country from Acre to Beirut, over the hinterland. It would take volumes, the old-style chronicles would say, to document the cruelties of the man. He cut down merchants and craftsmen and artisans and tribal shaykhs alike. He was an ambitious man, the lord of Acre. He hoarded the wealth of his province but wanted something to show for it: he repaired and adorned his capital city of Acre, renovated its ancient walls, built a solemn mosque (which towered over the walls), and a many-arched bazaar nearby.

Glory came al Jazzar's way in 1799, toward the end of his quarter-century in power, when Napoleon Bonaparte swept in from Egypt and laid siege to Acre. The French commander was on his way, or so it was thought, to Constantinople, and a dream of an eastern empire from Egypt to the Indus. Bonaparte had taken the very route to Palestine that the Crusaders had taken centuries earlier. The fort of Acre had been the seat of the Crusaders' last kingdom, the place where they had held out after their loss of Jerusalem. The siege had given al Jazzar his big role. Aided by a British naval squadron under the command of Sir Sidney Smith, his forces held out. The Frenchman's dream of an eastern empire was not to be. The governor had played on history's stage: those beaten villages and towns of the hinterland were no match for the ruler of Acre, who knew the intrigue of distant courts, the ambitions of larger powers. Decades and decades later, al Jazzar would still be remembered. His reign of terror would become a great divide between the grandeur of an imagined history and the bleakness and the supplication all around.

There were noble Arabian horses, but they had been replaced by donkeys and mules. In times past, men displayed their valor or fidelity by reciting poems and outdoing one another on special occasions. During weddings and funerals, my grandfather and a

few of his companions would ride to the village of Hula on paths so thick with vegetation that they had to lie flat on the backs of their horses for more than an hour at a time. Hyenas and jackals roamed the land around the vast swamps of Hula Lake. But Hula now lay across the border with Israel, a forbidden land. It had been drained long ago by Jewish farmers who tilled the land and wrestled with the malarial swamps. In the Hula of my grandfather's memory, the Jewish pioneers, men and women, worked the field side by side, and the women with bare thighs—thighs that the riders from our village glimpsed from afar and marveled at—were an intimation of another world.

There were rebellions and daring times when the Shia shaykhs and peasants of Southern Lebanon fielded ten thousand men with muskets. But the rebellions had been snuffed out, the muskets sold or confiscated. Now a mere corporal in the gendarmerie with two men by his side could have terrorized an entire village and taken men to Nabatiyya, the local seat of the government three kilometers away, to flog and interrogate them.

There was wealth in my village, wealth that supposedly belonged to us, but it was buried in jars never to be found again. The crafty ancestors had dealt their squabbling children one last unfair hand. They knew that as vitality and life slipped away, as they could no longer awe and intimidate their children, jars and deeds to land hidden away kept their sons and daughters reluctantly and grudgingly obedient. Hard as my aunts and my grandmother searched, the jars never turned up. In a dream it had been told that a jar was buried by the cool spring at the foot of the Crusader castle, Beaufort. But this dig, too, came to naught.

There were better things and better days. "Had you been around then, my dear child, you would have known who you were, and you would have seen something more than those

3

stunted tobacco plants and few fig trees." Almost a century before I heard of what it had been like and what we had once possessed, David Urquhart, a British traveler and diplomat, had come to this barren part of the country. "Have you music here?" he asked. "None; such things once abounded, but they are gone."

No one bothered to specify the time when the place knew a different kind of life. Men neither knew nor needed to know specific dates. They knew epochs and chunks of time and memorable events. The tales were part of men's lives—a world set alongside the backbreaking toil and the harsh earth, the stern fathers, and the capricious landlords.

—⁂—

I was the second son of Ali Ajami and Bahija Abdullah, a marriage that soon ended in divorce. My family's home was in Arnoun, in the district of Nabatiyya. The *hamma*, the entrance, of Arnoun was on the outskirts of the village. The houses there were owned by an absentee landlord, Riad al Solh, the scion of a family of wealth and standing with roots in Beirut and faraway Sidon. In his time, Riad al Solh had been a "big man," a prominent nationalist who had represented Beirut in Constantinople in the parliaments of 1909 and 1913 and had been a member of a short-lived Emirate of the Arab Kingdom of Damascus. In 1943, he had become the first prime minister of Lebanon.

But there was no sign of his presence: there were only the dogs of the *hamma*, the dogs of the overseer. These were a terror to the Arnounis. Making it past them was like the running of a gauntlet.

My mother had come to this ill-starred village when she married my father. The Abdullahs—her family—were a large clan

from Khiam, a town in the valley of Marjayoun. The distance to Khiam could not have been more than fifteen kilometers. But that was far enough to make it seem like a distant land. It was a place where children played next to running streams, and women had time to tell exquisite and drawn-out tales. The men working Khiam's fields retired to places in the shade; the exuberant women passing by gave more taunting and playful remarks than they received.

Arnoun, at the foot of Beaufort Castle and surrounded by granite cliffs, was a different kind of place, harsh and forbidding. There was to the place the feel of a quarry. Here the banter was less kind, the men more sullen and more brittle. The women struggling uphill to the wells, with jars on their heads, had little time or energy for chatter. There was a pond at the entrance of the village, by the gray mausoleum where my grandmother's parents were buried. But the pond that drew in the rain always dried up in no time. It was by its cracked, wrinkled surface that I knew the pond.

Arnoun lay on a high ridge. The hawks glided in from the valley below, carried by the wind, and circled the ridge, keeping watch over the shepherd boys and their flocks. Hyenas stalked the place. The dreaded creature, it was said, could cast a spell on its victims. But, as they also said in Arnoun, sons of Adam were more frightening than the hyenas. At the edge of the village, beyond its scattered patches of tobacco and its few fig trees, was the *wa'ar*, the wilderness. The *wa'ar* was more than a place beyond the village. It was a point beyond censure. It was from the *wa'ar*, the rocky, thorny land without vegetation, that the hyenas turned up. Stories were told of infants taken to the *wa'ar* who were never brought back. Daughters who dishonored their families were taken to the *wa'ar*. In the legend of the *wa'ar*, there was a rock

where a shepherd had killed his sister who had gone astray. He had taken her there, slit her throat, and left her to die. Years after that alleged deed, the Arnounis still swore they could identify the rock where the shepherd had done horror's work.

Ali Jamal, Ali the camel man, who led his camels by a small donkey to the distant villages of the Bekaa Valley and knew the surrounding hill country like the palm of his hand, had climbed the snow-covered peaks of nine-thousand-foot Mount Hermon. From its highest peak, one could see Damascus, ringed by its gardens, and Al Ghouta, with its poplar, sycamore, fig, and olive trees, surrounded by the vast Syrian Desert that stretched to the north. To the northwest was the plain of the Bekaa Valley, spread between a checkerboard of colors and patterns. To the south glistened the Sea of Galilee.

Ali Jamal, not a man of words, told the Arnounis one thing: theirs was a village with a special curse. He had not been precise, the camel man who always returned from his expeditions at dusk. He had not described other places and the ways of other people. But the Arnounis, who had no small measure of awe of Ali al Jamal, understood what he meant. Arnoun was a surly, hard village: the bay of distant hounds could be heard at night, the sun glared at midday, the unforgiving land sprouted tobacco plants everywhere. Ali al Jamal, who had seen the alleyways and cafés within Acre's walls, who had seen the waterfalls of a town just nestled in the hills beyond Arnoun, knew what he was talking about when he spoke of the curse of Arnoun.

Beaufort Castle

Then there was Beaufort Castle itself—long-ruined but ma-jestic and solitary atop the ridge, hanging at the edge of a vast precipice, some fifteen hundred feet above the bristling rapids of the Litani River, with the peaks of Mount Hermon in view. An Arab traveler and geographer said that Beaufort was set among the stars like a falcon's nest. But the Crusaders who had built Beaufort were anxious men. They built, we are told, when their confidence had been sapped, when the Latin Kingdom was in retreat and on guard. Their chroniclers tell us that from the par-apets of Beaufort the signalers could send their messages to the slopes of Mount Hermon, to the Castle of Toron, and to the coastal city of Sidon some thirty kilometers away.

A chain of seven fortresses, the chroniclers add, had been built to guard the frontier of the Latin Kingdom across the likeli-est invasion route from Damascus. It was a long route, a hundred

7

kilometers as the crow flies. Geographers of the place describe Beaufort as a spur castle: a fortress built on a rocky promontory at the junction of two gorges. The ridge, or spur, of such a castle has steep slopes on three sides, while the fourth, the saddle of the spur, is secured by a rock-cut moat. For all their brute strength, these castles were the work of pessimists, men seized with fear of living in open spaces. A chronicler who studied the spur castles, a geographer with no knowledge of the ways of Arnoun, might have been speaking of our tucked-away village when he observed that the people who had chosen Beaufort had chosen to shelter in "rocky clefts and behind stone walls like tortoises in their shells."

History had visited Beaufort. The Franks, the Crusaders, had held out in it after their defeat at the Battle of Hattin in 1187, at the hands of the great Muslim warrior, Saladin. A shrewd Orientalized Frank versed in Arabic, one Reginald of Sidon, attempted to negotiate the terms of its surrender after a year-long siege. Reginald, the native chroniclers say, had played tricks right to the very end. In Muslim hands, tied to a tree outside the castle walls, he exhorted his men on the inside not to give way, urging resistance while they were shooting arrows at him in order to put an end to his ordeal. Eventually the defenders were starved into submission.

The Franks would return some fifty years later. The Templars, a fierce order of monks and warriors, repaired the fortress, augmented its defenses, and built a Gothic hall in the central courtyard. But they were not to stay long. The Crusader venture had withered away by the final years of the thirteenth century. In 1268, the defenders of Beaufort were slaughtered after a short siege that lasted barely a fortnight.

Beaufort then slipped into obscurity. Over the centuries, soldiers would come every now and then: there were memories in

my village of Senegalese troops stationed in the castle, brought to this wilderness by the French in the interwar years, shortly before my birth. We were given no knowledge of what had brought the Senegalese to the ridge. Typically we were given no specific dates of their arrival. It was enough material for wonder that men of a different color had camped on the grounds of the castle and beyond its walls. There was a Syrian regiment that had come there two or three years after my birth, during the Arab-Israeli War of 1948–49. But Beaufort could not be befriended or owned. What had transpired behind its ruined ramparts on that ridge belonged to the dead. It evoked the dead among a people who dwelt on the dead and who spoke of them and who feared the unknown and what the world held in store for men. No one ventured close to the ruined castle after dusk.

—⟜⟝—

On the walls of my grandfather's house hung what passed for art and history—Persian miniatures whose subject was the eternal Shia theme of the persecutions of the imams by cruel caliphs and kings. In the Shia view the infallible imams were the legitimate successors and true heirs on earth to the Prophet Muhammad, his descendants through his daughter Fatima and her husband, Ali, also his cousin and beloved disciple. But the harsh world of politics was unfair to the imams, and history had become mere usurpation. In one of the colorful miniatures, the Imam Ali Rida is being offered poisoned grapes by the Abbasid Caliph al-Mamun. In the caliph's eyes, there was cunning and cruelty. And in the venerable imam's eyes, one could swear that one saw the serenity of a doomed man who knew what was in store for him. Eighth in line of the twelve imams of the Shia, Ali Rida knew

the history of his noble and doomed family. He knew how many of his ancestors had been poisoned and beheaded.

Mine were an insular people. The religion, with its tales of persecution and lament, was part of this insularity, this sense of being cut off from others. The miniatures alone gave us away as a people set apart from mainstream Sunni Islam. Sunni Islam, orthodox Islam, was an austere religion of the desert. It forbade visual representation of the Prophet and his family. It was the converted Persians—a more refined people than their Muslim Arab tribesmen conquerors, whom they had dismissed as lizard-eating men of the desert—who brought to Islam the miniature, the idea of ornament and art. Islam had overrun a feeble Persian Empire a few years after it outgrew its birthplace in the Arabian Peninsula. The Persians could not resist Islam. But they did the next best thing. They experimented with it and made it into their own. And in Shiism, a faith of embattled righteousness, they had found the proper vehicle, an outlet for their passion and their art.

The early Arab conquerors, the Prophet's political successors, had imposed Islam by the sword. What the Persians did was to adopt as their own the Prophet's family and its vanquished political cause. One descendant of the Prophet in particular, Imam Hussein, the Prophet's grandson, was adopted by the Persians as their own hero and icon. This descendant of the Prophet had been cut down by political rivals, murdered nearly half a century after the death of his grandfather. Persian legend made Hussein a man of Iran. Legend had it that he had married Shah-banu, the daughter of the last pre-Islamic Persian king. In the Persian rendition, Shah-banu had left Persia an innocent young woman. After her husband's death, she returned from the Arab provinces of Islam a woman made old before her time. The Persian passion, and the Persian grievance against the Arabian conquerors, had

taken away Hussein, as it were, from the Arabs. Shah-banu became the "mother of the nine imams" who came after Hussein. And the Persian artistic sensibility had rejected the strict orthodox Muslim ban on visual representations. The miniatures that adorned the wall in my grandfather's house were my first encounter with anything resembling art. Those miniatures spoke to a deep schism in the world of Islam between Arab and Persian, between the orthodox and the rebellious, between the austerity of Sunni Islam and the drama of Shia Islam, its sense of disinheritance and dispossession.

We knew the same tales as well. They were what set us apart from other Muslims. The history encroached on us, sat in our midst. It was there on the walls—severed heads, battles that raged far away and long ago. These tales of martyrdom were recounted for ten days of each year. Women chanted and wailed. Reciters supplied the searing details of what befell these sacred imams in Medina, in Iraq, in the northeastern Persian province of Khurasan.

Had there been books in Southern Lebanon, had Ahmad Pasha al Jazzar left the Shia libraries intact, the books would have elaborated the themes of the Persian miniatures in my grandfather's house. All the Shia books tell the tales of the twelve imams, the story of *ahl al bayt*, the Prophet's family; they all celebrate a grievance—virtuous men denied what was theirs, cruel men prevailing, history as usurpation.

The books tell, in endless variations, the story of Imam Hussein's journey from his home in Medina, the second holy city of Islam, and his stand at Kerbala, Iraq, in 680 AD against the unjust caliph; they tell how he perished and how he and his followers, cut off from the water of the Euphrates, gave their lives for a Muslim community that had gone awry. The imam had

fought a lone battle against a large army. The people of Iraq, who had invited him there to lead them against the humiliations and the oppressions inflicted on them by the troops of the ruler, had lost heart and had chosen to let the courageous man fight and die alone. The imam's words were preserved, and we memorized what he told the ruler's troops before the end came. Men took pride in his eloquence and coherence, and they told after the books and oral history, after the tales of reciters and grandmothers, of the devotion of Imam Hussein's sole surviving son, of the terrible fate that awaited so many of his progeny.

The large landholder who released himself of any social and political obligations, the fellow who walked out on an ailing wife for a younger woman, the loan shark who found a loophole around the religious ban on usury by giving his debtors a bar of soap at the conclusion of costly and exorbitant transactions—they all knew of the imams and of *ahl al bayt*. The honor of *ahl al bayt* was their story; and its misery and heroism embellished by the centuries was theirs as well. Their own ordeals and ambitions and the most searing experiences of their lives were expressed in its metaphors and its images. They had no better story to tell. No one in the Shia villages and towns of Southern Lebanon thought that any other drama could be as gripping or ennobling. Their own lives were outside the realm of investigation—small lives that didn't matter. Autobiographies, social inquiries, tales of men and women like themselves were something alien to their universe. The wisdom attributed to the imams was the stuff of books and miniatures and celebrations.

The characters in the tales of the imams were at times, it seemed, our contemporaries. All was said and understood when a divorced woman described her former husband as Shimar. In the legends and the books and the annual Passion Play in

Nabatiyya, the dreaded Shimar was the commander of the final assault against Imam Hussein. This was how my father was described by my mother. Um Fawzi, a tormented wife, knew no other way of describing her cruel and wily husband than to call him Yazid. Yazid was the Umayyad Caliph, the usurper who vanquished Hussein and humbled his family. A patient woman nearby, unlucky at every turn, reminded her friends and family of the fate of Zainab, Imam Hussein's sister, who died brokenhearted, wailing and lamenting for her noble family. Of a woman in the extended family, who was never without tricks up her sleeve and who seemed free of all scruples, it was said that she reminded everyone of Aisha. Aisha was the Prophet's strong-willed wife who, in the aftermath of the Prophet's death, took up arms against Imam Ali, campaigned against his succession to the caliphate, and acted cruelly and vindictively against her tender and virtuous step-daughter, Fatima. All sorts of rumors hovered over Aisha's reputation. She had once wandered away from the caravan and disappeared with a male companion. The Prophet, who accepted her tale of innocence and her claim that she had gotten lost, had exonerated her. But who knows? This modern-day Aisha, too, was a woman who lived under a cloud.

The great tale merged with the private lives here: Kerbala was never a faraway place by the Euphrates in Iraq or a battle that raged long ago. It belonged to the men and the women in Arnoun, people of the hinterland who were on the fringe of everything. They offered the tales of beheaded imams as personal metaphors and as public history, for their own history was denied them.

—⁓—

At the time of my birth, the village that lay at the foot of Beaufort was home to my grandfather, Shaykh Muhammad Ajami, to his wife, my grandmother Rawshna, the daughter of the Alawiyya family, and to their ten sons and daughters. My grandparents were a contrast. He was dark, exceedingly so, tall, and sturdy; she was short, bow-legged, with fair and smooth skin. He was a man of few words; she was a woman who kept a running commentary on the state of things. They were both of gentry background and means. My grandfather was a tobacco grower. The peasants of Arnoun toiled on one or two *dunams*, a quarter-acre, of tobacco. My grandparents had nearly thirty *dunams* of tobacco. The regulated licenses issued by the tobacco monopoly were even more difficult to come by than the land. Sharecroppers worked my grandparents' tobacco acreage and their other plots of land. Two shepherds tended to their herd of sheep and goats.

My grandmother's sense of her own class and distinction was passed onto her children. All were spared the toil of the land. The work was left to the sharecroppers and the *fellaheen*, the peasants of Arnoun. Promptings of a life beyond the land must have come early to the family: the children were provided elementary schooling in town; the dresses for the young women were made by the most skilled seamstress in Nabatiyya. My grandparents acquired a house in *Harat al Nasara*, the Christian quarter, of Nabatiyya. In the overwhelmingly Shia town, the Christian quarter stood apart from the rest. It was to the school run by nuns that my uncles and aunts went. My grandparents must have possessed an early sense of daring, some measure of courage in the face of the prohibitions and phobias about living with the *Nasara*. (In the family's memory, there is a priest somewhere in the background.)

The money from the land was taxed to the limits. It was always a struggle. Tobacco, the cash crop, had pushed aside other agricultural pursuits. And tobacco seemed like a crop with a curse. It had thrived here because the dry, hard earth favored the tobacco culture. What trees must have been there were cut down to make room for the tobacco plants. It was a monopoly item. The state—Ottoman and French rulers, then the Lebanese government—regulated it; the licensed monopoly, the *Régie des Tabacs et Tombacs*, estimated the tobacco yield of the land, assigned the price it saw fit, and fined those who delivered less than the estimate. No one here knew how to say the fancy words, "Régie des Tabacs et Tombacs." These were city words, words of Francophiles in Beirut. The people knew a single word, "Rogie," and pronounced it in their own peasant way. The feared and hated "Rogie" inspectors dined at my grandfather's home when they turned up in the winter. There was a single payday in the year when the Régie paid out for the crops it had taken. Throughout the year my grandfather borrowed money from loan sharks in Nabatiyya to keep the household in Arnoun intact.

My grandfather was born in Arnoun. The exact date of his birth was unknown. The date was fixed the way dates were fixed among a rural, largely illiterate population. He knew that he was born the year the Ottoman Sultan Abdul Aziz was murdered in faraway Istanbul. This puts the year as 1876.

His father, Dahir, had been a stranger who had come to this remote place from Tabriz some time in the mid-1850s. Tabriz was a city of disputation. A great drama had played out there shortly before Dahir had made his way to this remote village. A young merchant, one Sayyid Muhammad Ali of Shiraq, had proclaimed himself the *Bab*, the gate, to the Hidden Imam, the Lord of the Command. In his midtwenties, there had come to the

young merchant a special mission. In the esoteric sciences, and in his imaginings, he had found a deeper source of knowledge than that which was transmitted by the religious seminaries. There was in Shiism a central belief in redemption and in the imam, the guided one, who arrives at the end of time to bring justice to the world. The Bab appealed to this hidden yearning in Shiism and proclaimed himself the Promised One. He had not been religiously learned, but this had only enhanced his stature among the merchants and the artisans and the rebelliousness of the seminarians who had rallied to him. It had supplied proof that his gifts had come to him through divine intercession. The state and ulama had struck back: a special tribunal had been held in Tabriz to show the pretender the error of his ways. The tribunal asked the Shirazi merchant-saint to provide proof of his prophecy, miracles akin to those brought forth by other Prophets. The merchant-saint had brushed the challenge aside. He felt, he said, no compulsion to provide proof of his special gifts. The learned clerics had seen the tribunal as a chance to put an end to the pretender's movement, but it had been to no avail.

From simple beginnings, the movement of the Bab had become something the state and the orthodox mullahs of the land had to contend with, a gathering of free spirits. After some hesitation, a newly installed Shah authorized the execution of the Bab. The end came in the summer of 1850. On the day of his execution the Bab was taken by the authorities through the bazaar and the quarters to the barracks in the center of the city. The executioners were bent on humiliating the unrepentant rebel. His sash and gown and turban were removed; he was brought barefoot before a firing squad. With a disciple by his side, he was tied with a rope around a pillar. There would be something here, at the last moment, for the legend of the Bab. The first volley of bullets

struck the rope, and the Bab and his companion fell to the ground and disappeared into a room off the barrack's square. They were found by the troops, who did not miss the second time around.

Our last name, Ajami, meant the Persian. Dahir the Persian, or Dahir Ajami, had arrived here in the town of Nabatiyya with a group of fellow Persians. He left no recorded history. (My mother would never let that matter rest. She loved to remind my father's family that she, a woman of the lush valley just beneath the rocks of Arnoun, knew where her ancestors were buried, while the Ajamis were gypsies and vagabonds from the country of the Persians.) Dahir and his companions seemed anxious to bury their past. With the money that they had brought with them, the Persians put together new lives and married here. All of them, with the exception of two men, changed their Persian names to Arabic ones. One of the two settled in the town of Nabatiyya and took the Persian word *mirza*, or scribe, for a last name. In Persian, when mirza follows the name, it means a prince. It was the newcomer's chance: the scribe becoming a prince. The Mirzas became a prosperous family in Nabatiyya. When I was growing up, a Mirza was a physician in Nabatiyya and a friend of our family. Dahir the Persian did what insecure men did with money: he acquired land in this small remote village, among the rocks, in the shadow of Beaufort.

The years covered the trail Dahir took from Tabriz. No one bothered to inquire about the man who had left the city with its bazaar of five thousand shops, three hundred mosques, and one hundred public baths to come to Arnoun. In Dahir's time Tabriz was acclaimed as *Dar al'Sultanah*, "the abode of the Kingdom," "pinnacle of Islam." It must have been a city of one hundred thousand inhabitants. Travelers who went through the place spoke of its shade and its gardens, of its orchards of peaches and

apricots. Muslims and Armenians, Osmanli Turks and Persians, foreign missionaries and diligent students at the *talabiyya*, the Shia theological school, rubbed shoulders in its square and its alleys. *Vali ahd*, the crown prince, installed as Governor-General of Azerbaijan, lived in Tabriz doing what crown princes did—I suppose he mostly stayed out of the sovereign's way, kept his ears open to tales of intrigues and conspiracies, and inquired through trusted emissaries and agents in the capital about the sovereign's health, wishing his majesty, of course, nothing but the best of health. All sorts must have hung around the city: tricksters and con artists, sellers and buyers of spice, *sarrafs*, money changers, for commerce with Russia and Turkey, young men running away from military conscription, storytellers in coffeehouses running afoul of stern *mullahs* who disapproved of their art, old men sketching cabalistic diagrams and scribbling incantations for women anxious to ward off the evil eye from their children and their homes, to keep their husbands from falling into the snare of other women.

My great-grandfather traded all this for living in a quarry. After the death of his first wife, a widow from the town of Shaqlawa, Dahir brought his two children to this rocky hamlet. In his new land, he married into the Amins, a family of distinction in their small world. They were literati—clerics and scribes— and wrote books. His father-in-law was the sole landowner in Arnoun. The Amins had a recorded history. They were sayyids, meaning they claimed descent from the Prophet, and traced their roots back to Iraq. Several of them traveled between Shia Lebanon and Iraq and Iran, where they visited shrines and great religious seminaries, read rare old manuscripts, and kept diaries of their travels. Members of the family had served as jurists and clerics and educators. A marriage between Dahir from Tabriz and

Sakiba al Amin, my grandfather's mother, was a piece with the history of the family. Dahir came from Iran, a realm of the Shia faithful. The Amins took such matters seriously.

Years later I was to discover that Sakiba al Amin was a widow when she married Dahir. But I was to learn this in a biography of a mullah from the Amin family borrowed from the New York Public Library. My family kept it out of the family memory. Sakiba was remembered as just another bride from an illustrious town in the south, the daughter of a family of high religious calling.

Even though he was a man of the faith, Dahir's background must have set him apart in Arnoun. He likely came with a command of Azerbaijani, Turkish, and Persian. He no doubt spoke Arabic in the Persian way: a *wadi*, a valley, must have been a *vadi*; Imam Ali, wali Allah, trustee of God, must have been Ali vali Allah; the *wilaya* of Sidon, the province Sidon, must have been a *vilaya*. There has never been a Persian who was able to handle Arabic.

But Dahir's son, Shaykh Muhammad, spoke only Arabic, and he spoke it the way of other men of some means and distinction in Shia Lebanon. The Persian's son was a man of his village and his district. He even served as the *mukhtar*, the head-man or mayor, of Arnoun. His opponents had claimed that the election had been stolen from them, that the shaykh's men had tampered with the ballot box, that the shaykh should have lost by a good two dozen votes. But this, too, was a familiar tale of Lebanon, the only country that Muhammad, the son of Dahir, really knew and to which he fully belonged.

There is no way of knowing whether my grandfather yearned for, or even wondered about, his father's world. He had no memory of his father. Dahir had died when Shaykh Muhammad was only three years old. His mother, a woman of Southern Lebanon,

had taken him to Iraq for religious studies, a domain of her family. The resourceful widow wanted her son to take up her family's vocation. She entrusted him to a great religious scholar by the name of Muhsin al Amin, a relative of hers. But he was not to stay long in Iraq. Life in the religious seminaries was one of great privation in a cloistered world; the *taliban*, the students, invariably poor, with no means of their own, studied arcane material at the feet of masters, who provided them a small stipend (made possible by donations from the well-to-do) and rations of bread. This, the world of text and scripture, was not for him. Muhammad Ajami was his mother's pampered son, already a young man with an appetite for life; he loved his horses and his friends and his travels. He bade farewell to Muhsin al Amin and the great calling and returned home, never to look back with any fondness or nostalgia on the world of the seminaries. He returned with the title of shaykh—partially for his religious authority after having made the journey to Iraq and partially for his preeminence as a landlord. No surviving tale indicated that he had crossed the border into Iran, the land of his father's birth. No history was transmitted from father to son, no knowledge of what had brought him from Tabriz to Arnoun. No powerful bond united the two. What was there in Tabriz was left undisturbed— and unexplored. Curiosity was not part of the time and place. The world ended at a particular line. What was beyond the line was the concern of other men.

Much of Dahir's history went with him to his grave. But one particular tale survived. Dahir had left Tabriz with an older brother of his. They had parted company in Syria, in the great trading city of Aleppo. Years later, news came to Nabatiyya and Arnoun that Dahir's brother had settled in Aleppo and had been graced with success. Dahir made the journey to Aleppo to seek

his brother's help. Money was needed to purchase more land, to make ends meet. When Dahir located his brother in Aleppo, he found him leading the prayer at a large mosque, a deed reserved for men of distinction and learning. The older brother had passed himself off as a Sunni Muslim. The "Sunni" brother panicked when he saw the younger brother. The past had caught up with him. Aleppo was a zealous city of Sunni Islam, a fortress of orthodoxy. Some Sunni Muslims then still recalled that once upon a time it was more meritorious to kill one Shia than seventy Christians. In their eyes, the Shia were heretics. Disclosure would have been a ruinous affair. But Dahir was a subtle man; he waited and the two finally met under the cover of night in the other brother's home. It was a tender meeting. The older brother gave the help asked of him; in return he wanted to be left undisturbed in his new world, the past buried and over with. Dahir promised that there would be no return journey, no further pleas for help. He was to keep his promise: the Aleppine brother was swallowed up in the great life of the distant city. With the help given by the older brother, Dahir was able to build a house of stone in the center of Arnoun—a house with a courtyard, a thick vineyard, and its own cistern, bigger than the mud huts of the Arnounis.

My grandfather inherited the house and land in Arnoun. To be more precise, he inherited what land was left after Muhammad Maruni Alawiyya, a tax collector from a distant village in the district of Tyre, had schemed his way into dispossessing my grandfather's widowed mother of a portion of her land. Widows had a difficult time hanging onto what they inherited; they had to fend off relatives and tax collectors. Even a woman of steady nerves and will, a woman like Hajja Sakiba, had to part with a portion of her land.

The tax collector's daughter, Rawshna, was my grandmother. It was a bizarre beginning—the son of the dispossessed widow and the daughter of the tax collector. My grandparents' marriage was supposed to be a marriage of convenience, done to keep things quiet and peaceful in Arnoun, to make sure that some of the swindled land found its way back to the family. But there was more to it. This was a marriage Shaykh Muhammad Ajami wanted. He must have been about forty years old; she was a girl of fifteen.

In his younger years, my grandfather had sown his wild oats. Early in the twentieth century, during the harsh times of the Great War, he had gone as far away as Montevideo (Minat al Badawi was the way my grandmother pronounced it) in Uruguay. A dying empire—our Ottoman rulers—were going down in defeat. Crops were requisitioned by the governor of Sidon; in Nabatiyya merchants of grain were whipped in public for trying to conceal their supplies from the governor's troops. Legendary bandits of the parched villages, part thieves and part heroes, roamed the place, outwitting the oppressors. Then the locusts swept in from the sea and covered the sun, devouring what was left of the crops while helpless peasants set up fires to trap the waves of pests. Three hundred thousand people perished of hunger and disease. Burials had to be conducted by women because the men had given up and left. Amidst the troubles, my grandfather left to the New World.

In South America he had fathered a daughter he had left behind with her South American mother. He had married once, perhaps twice, again in Lebanon. It was easy for a landed man of standing to marry and divorce; he had indulged himself and savored his liberties. His wives in the old country had to contend with his mother, a strong-willed and bossy woman. They had not

been up to it. She had hounded and banished them. But he and his mother were to meet their match in the young daughter of the Alawiyyas. She was pretty and headstrong, "fair and plump," as the Shaykh described her, a young woman sheltered from the sun and field work. She came from a family of standing and plenty. She was not a young woman who had made her way to the well with an empty jar on her head or had packed the donkeys and the mules with clothes to be washed along the banks of the Litani River. She had never joined the women of Arnoun at the pond with her family's pots and pans.

Her five full brothers had inherited the cruelty and smugness—and ability to get government jobs—of their clever father, the tax collector. All were part of the feared *hukuma*, the government. The Alawiyya brothers reminded Arnoun's put-upon peasantry of Turkish officialdom. They had the fair skin and the overbearing mannerisms and the language of officialdom. All five had been sent to Istanbul for education, where two had finished an officers' training course in the military academy. The Alawiyyas believed in their right to things and their right to command.

Her father, now deceased, had left her a good deal of land, and she had many suitors. A suitor from the nearby town of Nabatiyya, it turned out, had brought the young daughter of the Alawiyyas to Shaykh Muhammad's attention. The Nabatiyya man had asked for the shaykh's help and mediation with Rawshna's mother. My grandfather had not thought that young Rawshna was ready for marriage. But with the bid of the man from Nabatiyya, Shaykh Muhammad took a second look and liked what he saw. The would-be intermediary put in his own bid.

There would be no other wives for the man who had gone to Montevideo; he would never stray far again. He was smitten by

the young wife. Hajja Sakiba, his bossy mother who had thought that the young daughter-in-law would give her, the mother-in-law, a decided edge, would live to learn of the formidable will of Rawshna Alawiyya, who would come into the marriage with the self-confidence born of wealth and good looks and status. In no time, Rawshna would prevail, and Hajja Sakiba would storm out of Arnoun never to return. She joined her three married daughters in the town of Khiam, in the valley of Marjayoun, where she died and was buried, having spurned her son's efforts to conciliate her. Rawshna was left the undisputed mistress of her domain and her village.

My grandmother may have been the daughter of a scoundrel, the sister of capricious souls who never did anyone a favor, but she fended for herself and earned her place. She gave birth to eleven children, four boys and seven girls, in a childbearing cycle that spanned two decades. The eldest, my uncle Hussein, was born in 1918. The youngest, a girl, was born in 1938, some five years before my brother's birth and seven years before mine. My father, Ali, their third child, was the first to have his mother's reddish hair and fair complexion.

Ten of Shaykh Muhammad and Rawshna's eleven children survived to adulthood—a remarkable thing for the time and the place. Only one, my Aunt Raqiyya, died a young girl. An old, grainy black-tinted photograph of her hung in my grandparents' living room, right next to the Persian miniatures commemorating the battles and deaths of virtuous Shia imams. The photograph is of a child around ten years of age, with soft eyes and her mother's complexion. It was by Raqiyya's memory that vows and promises were made. It was by the sacred soil of Raqiyya's grave that a story received its alibi as a truthful one. A decade after her death, Raqiyya lived in the memory of her sisters and brothers,

in the imagination of nephews who had never seen her. It was said that she had been happy to have her new sister-in-law Bahija Abdullah around and that she loved her first nephew, the first grandchild to be born, my brother Riad. Stories were told about how she had sat by his crib and sung lullabies to him.

—⁓—

My Aunt Raqiyya was too young to concern herself with something that greatly agitated my grandmother Rawshna: my mother had come to the Ajami family after a failed first marriage in a neighboring village. The woman from Khiam may have taken pride in her town and her own pedigree, but she was already a "woman" when she married into the Ajamis. (There were "girls" and there were "women"; girls were virgins, women were not.)

My mother had come to Arnoun from her beloved town in the valley via another rocky hamlet nearby, the village of Jibshit. A sayyid, a descendant of the Prophet, had come to her father's home in Khiam and had wanted her for his wife. My mother was then a young woman of seventeen in her father's home. Running time back as on a reel, I could see what the sayyid saw: a young woman about five feet tall, slightly plump, with white skin, high cheek bones, auburn hair streaked with red henna color. Her color and her shape were close to her society's notions of beauty. Fair women were what everyone wanted for a daughter, for a wife. These were superstitious people: they brooded and they worried. The world brought them very few pleasant surprises. A dark face, they feared, ushered in a dark day. No husband toiling the miserly land and worrying about capricious officials who always came for plunder, no family trying to keep its world intact wanted the

misfortune associated with a dark face. White skin and fair hair were the emblems of fortune and authority.

The fair-skinned daughter of the Abdullahs was no doubt talkative. All the Abdullahs were talkative and encouraged their daughters to speak their minds. I could easily imagine a touch of stridency in her when she was a girl in the home of her father. He was a man of gentle disposition. I imagine he indulged her independent spirit.

As befitting a young woman who had options, who lived in a valley, who had many brothers and a father with some land, who was reluctant to go far from her proud town to a small village, my mother had objections to the marriage. Sayyids were a peculiar lot: there was a touch of madness, of eccentricity in them. Somehow sayyids grew up twisted, bearing a special burden, existing in a twilight, in a no man's land between a harsh environment that denied everyone and a claim of their own distinction and sacred lineage.

Sayyids were entitled to respect. But irreverent young women like my mother still had opinions on their suitors. I know my mother was not particularly impressed with the sayyid. His looks may have failed to move her. Secluded women in the cities of the Muslim world may have been traded, bargained over, between fathers of would-be brides and their suitors. But these were not the ways of the people in my mother's world, peasantry or gentry. Women mingled with men here; they entered into battles of wits with them. There was no seclusion when the sayyid came courting. My mother must have told him, in her rich and emphatic vocabulary, to go back to his wretched village of Jibshit where people were hungry, where no guest was ever given a decent meal. Word had come to Khiam that the sayyid had a difficult mother, miserly and cruel, a woman who could never bring herself to fry

an egg for a visitor let alone slaughter a chicken in his honor. The sayyid's mother lived with him. Any bride that came in would have to battle the older woman over the produce of the land, over the attention and ear of the man of the house.

My mother had her doubts. But the sayyid persisted. He offered a generous bride-price that had two parts. One part, *muqaddam*, was what was paid in advance; the other, *muakhkher*, was what was promised if the marriage broke down. The Abdullahs, and similar families with daughters given into marriage, did not quibble over the advance payment. They were not selling their daughters; they did not need to. As they put it, they were not sitting around waiting for someone to feed them or take their daughter off their hands. They asked for a nominal gift to be provided in advance. They did quibble, however, over the *muakhkher*. They made it as steep as they could. Men tired of women or changed their minds. They were lured away by younger women. Sometimes, even in his old age, a lecherous old man had a second wind and walked away from a wife of many years, making a fool of himself and his family. Deferred bride-price, the *muakhkher*, was an insurance policy, a way of staying men's passions, or at least of making them pay for their change of heart.

The Sayyid of Jibshit offered sufficient land. And he found an ally in my mother's mother. A marriage to a man of such holy descent brought *baraka*, a blessing, to the entire household. An older brother of my mother was also persuaded. The headstrong young woman's objections to the sayyid had not been unduly violent or strong. She was really straddling the fence. The objections were there, but they were of the kind that could be worn down, and they were.

Hers was a wedding worthy of the young daughter of the Abdullahs. Years later, she still remembered the neighing of the

proud white mare she rode on that day, the boisterous village band that accompanied her on her procession, the elaborate meal that was served, the ululation of the Abdullah women. She could see on that day that the villagers of Jibshit were a timid, surly lot. She could see it in the way the women refused to join the *dabkeh*, the folk dance, and in the stunted, hesitant way the men danced the *dabkeh* when they joined in, dragged in against their will by the proud young men of Khiam. She could see it, too, in the somber dark colors of the dresses of Jibshit's women on a day that the Abdullah women wore their brightest colors.

She was leaving a lush valley for a brooding village, but she trusted her fate to the Almighty and to the unknown and to her heady belief in herself. She had no doubt that she would prevail in the test of wills against the sayyid's mother, and that she would bring some of Khiam's ways to the rocky hamlet where fate had consigned her.

But all was not well in the sayyid's home. My mother clashed with her mother-in-law. Our older people had very strong opinions. Their opinions were the products of habit, of innate pessimism. And with time the habits took the shape of an unassailable and sacred order of things. Things that were so fine that they were hard to fathom struck them as matters of great importance. My mother did not fit in the sayyid's mother's scheme of things. The older woman wanted submission. But submission was not something that my mother was good at. She had not been brought up to submit.

The sayyid's home had known little laughter and very few visitors before my mother's arrival. My mother brought with her Khiam's passion for long evenings, its pride in hospitality. More trips had to be made to Nabatiyya to stock up on rice and sugar. The grain and the flour stored at home were depleted by the new

wife at a rate that the older woman in the house took as a sign of future ruin for the sayyid.

The unhappy marriage lasted six or seven years. It had produced three children. The firstborn was a daughter, a bad omen. The second was a boy, the sayyid's first son. Then another daughter came. Several times my mother had stormed out and returned to her town and her people. The sayyid came and pleaded with her to return with him to Jibshit. Promises were made that his mother would become more tolerable. But nothing changed after each reconciliation. Troubles erupted again. My mother must have been beaten once or twice. Men did such things. Such things needed no sanction. The cruel sayyid had to be careful though. My mother had brothers, and one of them was a fiery-tempered man who was not to be trifled with. The Abdullah woman was not a socially isolated, helpless woman.

The men in my mother's household—her father, her two brothers, the older gentle one, and the younger troublesome one—accepted her verdict that her marriage had been ruptured. They saw to it that the deferred bride-price, two or three pieces of land, was paid up. In the household of my mother's father, no great shame was attached to the failed marriage in Jibshit. Fate had played its hand. Their daughter had rejected the sayyid's ways and returned to Khiam. But no measure of family support could completely wipe the slate clean. Divorce was a rarity then. This was the family's first experience with divorce. A girl had returned a woman. The three children had to be left in Jibshit, in the custody of the father. Henceforth, Bahija Abdullah could not be as strident, as sure of herself. The second time around there was to be no wedding, no white mare strutting to the music of the village band, no memorable meal.

It was a quiet, subdued affair, a marriage contracted in the face of the opposition of my father's mother. Ali had always been his mother's boy, her pride and joy. She had wanted for him a normal marriage. Of all her sons, he was the one whose looks she had admired and taken pride in. She had anticipated the excitement of looking around for a suitable bride, the power that would be hers as the anxious mothers of marriageable young women awaited her decision and sought her approval. She had done a fair amount of scouting around. There were proud households in neighboring villages who had daughters with decent dowries, good families keen to see their daughters to their right and honorable station in life. God had willed a different outcome; Ali brought into the household a divorced woman who was not showing proper contrition over her first failed marriage. The Abdullah woman brought into this second marriage the land she had acquired when the sayyid had divorced her. She surrendered the deed to the plots of land to the younger man she had married. Rawshna's narrative had skipped that detail. The land was sold, and the money from it had been spent. Bahija Abdullah never forgot the day she had surrendered her deed to the land, initialed the transaction with a red thumbprint before the provincial clerk in the town of Nabatiyya. The land had been protection, a hedge against an uncertain world, to be kept for a "black day." But the die was cast. Her husband had wild notions of what he would do with the price of the land, of the doors the money would open. He knew she wanted out of his parent's household. He promised her the break she wanted. He might have even promised a move to Beirut as soon as the land was sold.

Ali, may he be lost to the world and may his mother grieve for him, had married a divorced woman six or seven years older than he was. The wife had delivered a child. But now with a woman

and a child in his father's domain, claimants to what little there was to be claimed, Ali was coming and going between Arnoun and Nabatiyya. In Nabatiyya he had fallen for a younger woman. Of his wife in Arnoun he now said that the whole thing had been an error of his youth. In a moment of innocence, a young man had married an older woman. The Devil tested men, played with them; the Devil came in the form of a woman. "Their malice is great," some religious saying or scripture had said of women.

There was a Ford Model T that took the people of Arnoun to Nabatiyya. On Mondays, the day of the market, Haidar, the Ford owner and driver, did a brisk business, packed in his passengers. The younger men with bravado preferred to ride on the car's running board. Most of the villagers came cowed to Nabatiyya; they were on their best behavior, dressed in their best attire. They came to buy tins of *halva*, cans of sardines, some flour, a kilo-gram or two of sugar. The truly lucky ones strutted to the meat market where the butcher grilled exquisite skewers of lamb. For the others, the smell of the grilled meat just played with them, tormented them.

Other Arnounis came to Nabatiyya only on Monday. But Ali, the son of Shaykh Muhammad, could be relied upon to make the trip other days of the week as well. Arnoun was his father's universe, the home of his wife and child. Ali felt at home in Nabatiyya and wanted out of Arnoun and his marriage.

"How is your mother?" was asked of him in Nabatiyya. The reference was to my mother, his older wife. My mother was living on borrowed time. In the first marriage, divorce had been her own choice: the panic and frenzy of the second failure was wholly different. Years later, she could still break down when this subject came up. She went back over it again and again. There was no structured narrative—only the hurt and the humiliation of it all.

A few times, she had trailed my father to Nabatiyya, to the hated house in the unlit alleyway in Hay'al Saraya, the Alley of the Serial, where my mother's rival lived with her divorced mother and divorced aunt. My mother attributed dark, demonic powers to the house in Nabatiyya. It was there where the threads of her ruin were being spun. She had no answer for the charms of the house in the Alley of the Serial: a trap had been laid for the young restless man, and he had taken the bait. Behind him was the other wife and the unforgiving village and the father who eyed him and his comings and goings with quiet but obvious disapproval. She was beaten two or three times. The young man in the great town of Nabatiyya went at the wretched past that chased him with fury. Each time my mother walked back the distance to Arnoun, she returned to the consoling presence of her first child—and to the imams entrusted with protecting defeated women and abandoned children, and to the household work that awaited her.

My mother's rival must have been a young woman of sixteen. My mother was then thirty. One woman's life was behind her, the other's had promise. The younger woman talked of time spent with her father in Venezuela, of the few words of Spanish she had known. The father had since divorced her mother, the few words had been forgotten. Still, the advantage she had in her youth and looks in the eyes of the restless man must have been staggering; there was no way the older rival could have withstood that sort of challenge. No great gap in manners had yet opened between "modern" and "traditional" women. The world here had not yet awakened to pretensions. But there were differences between the two women that a young, restless man contemplating a move to the city—pushed off the land by a stern, disapproving father, by crops that yielded enough to make ends meet but left no margin for choice—could see and could appreciate.

A break came my mother's way. It must have been the out-come of the constant prayers and the tears. The imams must have come to her rescue. At dusk, news came to the straw hut under my grandfather's fig trees where my mother loved to spend sum-mer nights, that my father had been arrested smuggling guns to Palestine. The news was brought back by a companion of his who had escaped arrest. The guns had come from a Greek in the French Foreign Legion, Nicholas or Nichola, as he was called here, who had escaped from his unit stationed at Beaufort.

Nichola wanted to go back to his beloved Greece. He deserted and sought help. My father, on the lookout for opportunities, had offered it. But Nichola had to pay his way, had to make offering him a place to hide worth the risk of running afoul of the French army. Nichola brought some stolen rifles in the deal.

But Arnoun was a small place: there were too many eyes, too many people hoping that a word to the authorities would bring a small reward—some bread, a discarded pair of boots, a few pias-ters. And, besides, there were always men who cut off the escape routes of others, who tried to deny them what little opportunity presented itself because nothing of consequence was happening in their own lives. The movements and the comings and goings of those who tried, the lucky, were a threat to men who had so little. A successful man made the misery of others suddenly unbear-able: things lived with and endured became shameful, a source of great rage, when another man braved the limits, turned up with new money, strutted around with new evidence of success. Men lived in the eyes of others: they compared, they envied. They feared what a man would do with his luck.

Nichola was turned in. He had hidden in my grandfather's home, in a barn that he shared with piles of chaff and two cows. His kindness to the whole family, especially to my infant brother,

became part of our tales and our memory. Nichola had said that one day he would take the young child to Greece, home of all learning and science. This Greek, this stranger, had complimented my mother, a woman being forsaken by her husband. His kind words were remembered.

Nichola, it turned out, was a man of fidelity. He did not turn my father in. But my father had anticipated things and had taken the rifles across the border to Palestine. The episode would become part of his legend: he made the journey at night, dodging the "chasseurs Libanais," a troop of cavalry who patrolled the frontier between Lebanon and Palestine, by listening for the hooves of their horses. He also had to be careful about the Senegalese troops, who were known for cruelty and shot smugglers and drifters on sight. Metullah, the old Jewish settlement across the frontier, was his destination. He knew Metullah. He had carried on some small trade with the settlers in the past. It was a bumper crop that year, and the fields of wheat and barley along the way gave him some cover. The luck that saw him through on one side of the frontier, though, failed him on the other. On the outskirts of Metullah, he was picked up by the British.

This was 1944, before the time of large nationalist judgments, before those who went across the border and dealt with the Jews, the *Yahud*, of Palestine were labeled as traitors. Nationalism did such things: it declared things impermissible, gave them new names, and endowed them with morality and immorality. But this morality had not yet come to Arnoun. My father was probably selling guns to the Palestinians, but he could have been doing it for the other side. Men crossed the border to buy and sell what was there to be bought and sold. What mattered was the ability to go across the border, to return with something to show for it, to flaunt one's will and success, to outdo one's siblings.

It was known in these parts that the *Ingliz*, the British, looked unkindly on the trade in contraband arms. A few years earlier, a barbed wire fence had been put up on the border between Lebanon and Palestine: our French rulers on one side, the *Ingliz* on the other. The *Ingliz*, caught between Arab and Jew, were riding a tiger. Weapons brought into Palestine by small-time gunrunners complicated their task. Promises had been made to the *Ingliz* that the border would be sealed. Cavalry and gendarmes were recruited on our side of the border to control the traffic in arms. But no gunrunner worth his name, no son of a free woman, could fail to strike a deal with the gendarmes or to elude them.

The news delivered to the straw hut was a relief. Perhaps God had answered my mother's prayers. Ali Ajami, my mother hoped, could be imprisoned for a year or two. She would remain amidst his family, his wife in God's eyes. And who knows: the errant husband might return from prison a changed man. Men were strange beings. Obsessions seized them and then let go of them. Magic spells could be cast on them by scribblers of strange incantations, amulets stuffed under their doorsteps could blind them—but the spells could be broken, and the blinded ones could be released. Men were cruel, but they were fickle and malleable. A year or two of jail could conceivably reform him. He might forget the road to Nabatiyya. Or the young woman in Nabatiyya could ensnare someone else, and the errant husband would then put the whole thing behind him.

My grandmother Rawshna had seen my mother interrupting the baking of bread, taking off her headscarf, and lifting her hands to heaven. Rawshna knew what the prayers were about: "Bahija, I know what you are doing. You are praying for my son's imprisonment. But when Ali returns I will be sure to tell him of

your happiness with his misfortune. It will be the last straw. I shall be there to remind you of what I said."

At times, mighty powers intervene and deliver solitary souls from impossible situations. More often, the world is as small as it is and hell a private matter that belongs to a solitary individual and refuses to be shared. My mother's faith in the imperial power of the *Ingliz* was misplaced. The *Ingliz*, the mighty *Ingliz*, had big things to worry about, bigger things than a small-time gunrunner. Those who knew things knew that the *Ingliz* were close to giving up, that they were about to pack up and leave Palestine to an all-out fight between Arabs and Jews. They no doubt saw the young man in their hands as just another desperado, another native of the land. He must have been afraid. He must have promised he would never return to Palestine. The fury with which a wife was beaten, the power with which a child, his firstborn, was flung out of his crib, the thunder at home in Arnoun—all these must have failed him on that day when he stood in the presence of the *Ingliz*. His reddish complexion may have awed a peasant woman in Arnoun or intimidated a sun-charred peasant working his land. But the *Ingliz* were not impressed. They imprisoned him for a month. Then they took him to the border and let him go.

"My dear Bahija, you must have gloated over my absence; you must have wished that I was lost somewhere in Galilee or that I vanished in the prisons of the Ingliz. But I am back. All these intercessions, all these prayers were to no avail."

The gunrunner, the outwitter of the *Ingliz*, returned home on a hot, still night in summer. Years later, my mother still recalled the details of his return. She was sleeping on the rooftop of my grandparent's home, next to a large spread of figs that had been put out to dry before they were stored away for the winter seasons. Sleeping by her side was her son. At the *hamma* the dogs of Riad

Bey al Solh barked and snarled into the night, trailing and then giving up on the person who had disturbed the peace of their domain. An Arnouni, a peasant who had come back from Palestine the day before to my grandfather, had brought home the news that Ali had been let go.

Umm Abbas, my mother's friend, a woman who sympathized with the daughter of the Abdullahs for coming from far away and for being thrown amidst a people with no mercy, assured my father that he "filled his wife's eye," that he was "the best of men," that everyone was happy to have him back. Faithful Umm Abbas volunteered to take the child away. He had asked to have his son sleep next to him on his return from Palestine. But both Bahija Abdullah and Umm Abbas said that it would be best if the child stayed at Umm Abbas's. After all, Ali had made a long journey, had fought the battles of men; women had ululated for him, celebrating his triumphant return. He had vanquished the *Ingliz* and disappointed the ill-wishers. The child would disturb his sleep.

In truth, Bahija Abdullah and Umm Abbas never trusted Ali Ajami with his firstborn.

Children, our people said, were the adornment of life and of this world—*Zinat al Hayat wa al Dunia*. They said it in the way they recited things, without thinking about it. The saying had come to them. They repeated it. Everyone said it.

But infants were found dead in their cribs. Small children fell off the low roofs of the mud huts and the houses of stone during summer nights when figs were put out to dry. A man contemplating opportunities, a man pressed against the wall, was capable of doing anything. Even Ali Ajami's father worried about the cruelty of Ali toward his firstborn. He wondered if it went beyond the healthy dosage of our people's cruelty toward children. There

were hushed stories in Arnoun of Ali and Bahija's firstborn. There were doubts about the child's chance of survival.

"Bahija, daughter of the Abdullahs, you must not hallucinate, you must not tell wild stories about Ali Ajami and his first child. So he wanted the child by his side when you slept on the rooftop, and he once flung the child out of his crib. You can't let your imagination run wild with such tales, tales about you coming from the *tanoor* to find the infant's head under a pillow. It is true that Ali never shows his first child any affection. But look at his father, Shaykh Muhammad: the shaykh fathered eleven children and never showed any of them 'an atom's worth' of affection. A father never pampers children in this hard world. A man gives a child his name, propitiates outside powers, does the work of the land, smuggles guns to Palestine, teaches his sons the words and duels of men, hounds him to do his best. Besides, Ali is a hounded man, chased by his own demons, by the young woman he desired, by all those unfulfilled dreams of the things he wanted, of the freedom he had never had."

My father had declared that he was through with my mother. He was talking of divorce. He was clearly on his way to Nabatiyya. But I, the second child born to Ali Ajami and Bahija Abdullah, gave him away. A cholera epidemic struck the villages of Southern Lebanon in 1945, the year of my birth. Like a yellow wind, it streamed through the blighted villages, carrying away the weak and infirm and unhealthy. But I managed to survive. Ali, may his mother grieve for him and give his name to his second born, had weakened again. He had burdened himself and his father's household with a second child. Women were good at spinning webs for men, it was said in Arnoun. This was said by my grandmother. No sooner had a man broken through one web than another was spun. My mother had tricked her husband yet another time.

But my mother's webs were not sturdy enough. My arrival did not save the marriage of cruelty and unhappiness. Soon after my birth, my father was on his way to Nabatiyya and to a second marriage. His quiet father summed up his disapproval and his exasperation in a few short words: "From Bahija to Khadija." The devil came in the form of two women.

—⁓—

When my parents' marriage ended, or to put it in more appropriate terms, when the son of Shaykh Muhammad finally divorced the daughter of the Abdullahs, my mother chose to stay in Arnoun. My mother had walked away from her family and her town to cast her fate with my father's family. When the remarks of my aunts were unusually cutting or the household demands of my grandmother unduly harsh or when a woman married to an uncle of mine taunted her about her failure to keep a man, my mother walked to the edge of my grandfather's vineyard and, looking across the gorge, so many kilometers away, she would situate Khiam and speak to her loved ones. On the far horizon the snow-covered peaks of Mount Hermon, shining brilliantly in the daylight, bounded the world. But she would raise her hands to heaven and ask God to punish the man who had rejected her for a younger woman. "Ali Ibn Rawshna, Ali the son of Rawshna, there will be an account between us in front of holy and just imams, in a different world." This done, she hurried back, past the thistles and the untended vineyards and the fig trees and the straw hut on stilts that my young uncle had put together for summer nights, to what she had at hand, for she knew so well that for her there was no way back to the crisp chatter of Khiam. She had run out of options. The first failed marriage could be written off and excused.

The second one had delivered a final judgment. My mother clung to my brother and me with a passion that had to do with the guilt over the first marriage, over the first three children. She stayed in Arnoun by our side, with my father's family.

My grandfather was an honorable man. He and my grandmother may have regretted my birth, but blood was thicker than water. The madness of his son was one thing, the fate of two grandsons quite another. I was of them. I became part of their burden and their world and their fate. My brother, my mother, and I shared in what the land gave.

My father wanted to wash his hands clean of the whole thing, of the responsibility for two sons. He railed against the cruel fate that had robbed him of his youth, against the load he would have to carry without access to the many roads that would otherwise be open to him if his whole wretched marriage, and the two children who came with that marriage, were not in his way. My grandfather was to block him at every turn. The older man was still held by shame, by pride, by the ethic of the land, by the sense of some superior power that judged men and that one day meted out either punishment or favor to them. My father was attempting to release himself from the limits and the prohibitions of his world. The younger man's fury, his sense that he deserved more elbow room, more freedom from the hold of his elders and the obligations to his children, put him beyond shame and pity—never as far as he may have wanted, but far enough to give a license to a good deal of absolution and freedom.

There was another bond that my grandfather honored and that worked to my mother's advantage. All three of my grandfather's sisters, his sole surviving family, were married to Abdullah men from Khiam. News of my mother's ordeal spread to Khiam. Word came back that the Ajamis of Arnoun were a heartless

lot. The marriage between Shaykh Muhammad's son and Bahija Abdullah had failed. Such things happened. But what of the honor of Shaykh Muhammad? He had his daughter-in-law and his two grandsons at home. The shaykh could not save the marriage. But he could show his mettle in the way the two grandsons and their mother were treated. My grandfather knew that men judged harshly in his world, that a man's reputation was his most valuable possession.

My mother reminded my grandfather of something else he knew. Sons were capricious and could do what they wanted. They could get away with cruelty. He had four of them. But the shaykh had six daughters of his own. Men who tormented other men's sisters, other men's daughters could live to experience the same fate befalling them. The unseen hand of vengeance had a way of settling accounts. My mother and the patriarch of Arnoun had between them the sensibility of their world and its prohibitions. They were brought together in the fight to feed and educate us— and to cut off my father's route of escape.

My mother, now a former daughter-in-law, pulled her weight in Arnoun. She did what work there was to be done. Bread had to be baked. The thistles and thorns covering my grandfather's vineyard had to be cleared. Dry weeds and thorn bushes had to be found for the fire. Clothes had to be packed on mules and taken on a rocky path to the Litani River for washing. Olive trees had to be shaken and the olives picked up, brought home, pounded with wooden hammers, and put away to ripen in jars of glass or taken to the *ma'serah*, the olive presser, in Nabatiyya to be pressed into oil. Pots and pans had to be taken to the pond at those times of the year that the pond had water in it. There was a grinding handmill in my grandfather's house—a handmill for the grain, as

old as time, with a handle and two millstones. My mother worked that handmill for hours at a time.

My early memories of her, those that come and offer themselves, are memories of her by the handmill, or at the pond, or during those excursions to the Litani River that I waited for with great anticipation. The descent to the Litani was always a one-day affair. The donkeys were loaded with clothes for the steep scramble to the river. We made camp on its bank by a spot where the river was calm, and its color was a deep, clear blue. The women built a fire with the thistles, which were hauled to the clearing from the rocky hills; the clothes were boiled in large aluminum pots, then rinsed in the river and put out to dry in the sun over the shrubs and the rocks. The work done, the women bathed in the river, washing their hair with large, hard bars of soap. Because we had not been taught to swim, and we were not permitted to venture far, we feared the river and hung close to the bank.

My mother had a melodic and lush voice and a store of lullabies and songs—now and then a light song, but more often songs of lament about fate, *al Dahr*, and its ways. The women of Arnoun, working by her side, joined in, broke into the hymns that they knew, or simply added the chorus's words of appreciation, the stock words of our songs of lament. My mother was good at improvising her own hymns and songs as she went along. The songs, the ear for music, and the rhythm must have been the gifts of the valley.

My mother stayed in Arnoun for as long as possible. My father had by then found his way to the outskirts of Beirut and had started a small private elementary school in an Armenian ghetto northeast of the city. We had to go to school, and there was no schooling to be had in Arnoun. But more than schooling was at stake. We had outgrown the land in Arnoun. It was time, too, for

my uncles and aunts to make the passage to Beirut. A generation earlier, in 1931 or 1932, they had attempted a first passage to Beirut. They rented a house in the middle of an orchard to give the city a try. Much yearning and ambition must have gone into this journey. The boys were sent to a decent school, the oldest of the girls to the celebrated lycée of the *Mission Laique Française* in the Zokak el Blat quarter in West Beirut. Shaykh Muhammad and Rawshna no doubt had sunk good money into this attempt. My grandfather had contracted a sudden romance for the city. He thought of buying a car, hiring a driver, recasting himself into a man of Beirut. But that passage had not worked: the raw nerves of the countryside, the Shia sense of separateness, had failed them. In the great city there was only a scant Shia presence then: an isolated band of families with no cemeteries or mosques of their own. At that time, the dead among this community had to be taken back to their ancestral villages. Amidst the settled Sunnis of West Beirut, their confidence had cracked; the house and the orchard were given up, the sons and daughters of Shaykh Muhammad and Rawshna returned to the south and to the schools of Nabatiyya.

This second passage, some fifteen years later, was for good: there would be no return to the land, no tale of a pretty house and a lost orchard. There were five daughters to worry about. It would be easier to find them husbands in Beirut. Abbas, the youngest of the shaykh's four sons, was showing some promise at school and had gone beyond what the provincial town of Nabatiyya could offer. The city had changed for the good in the intervening years. Other brave families from the Shia hinterland had begun to stake their claim to their fragments of the city. Rashid Bey Beydoun, a stylish Shia notable who wore his fez at a rakish angle and seemed free of the timidity of his people, set out to give himself and his

sect a place in the city. He built a secondary school and a mosque for his people in West Beirut; he established a philanthropic association. The ambitious politician knew his city. He assembled a group of *qabadayat*, street toughs, who were ready to do his bidding. Such were the rules of the city: if *Basta*, the Sunni quarter, had its *qabadayat*, so would Rashid Beydoun and his people. He gave his men a grand name: *talaya*, the vanguard. They had more bark than bite, the boys of the *talaya*. But the timid men and women of the hinterland saw in Beydoun and his men and his school the beginning of their emancipation. It was in the school established by Rashid Bey Beydoun that Abbas was to enroll.

A generation earlier it had been my grandmother who had fled back to the countryside. She was no more reconciled to the city this time around, but she would not get her way this time. Had she been overruled back then, the landing of our clan in the city would have been much easier. We would have had a head start. My aunts and uncles and my father would have learned the ways of the city: they would not have had to do it in so frenzied a way when they came a generation later. The city would have seeped into them, softened them. The city itself was beginning to shed its old ways then. Its settled Muslim families themselves were groping for a way of life beyond the old limits. It was in the late 1920s that Saniyyah Habbub, the first Muslim woman to attend the American University, had arrived, fully veiled on the cable car, to the campus of the American University. She had walked through the main gate before removing her veil and partaking of the liberty that the sanctuary of this institution built by American missionaries afforded her.

My mother was quick to follow: she brought us to the same Armenian ghetto in Beirut where my father had come. For a peasant woman, the fear of the unknown and the awe of what

the city held in store had to be balanced against the merciless village she knew. When she set out for Beirut, my mother, then in her mid-thirties, had only known the remote villages of the south. Her world had been limited to her town in the valley and to the two villages into which she had married. What lay beyond the mountains and the hills that bordered her world was of no concern of hers. A stone's throw from her small world there was the coastal city of Sidon. It was midway to Beirut, a place where the bare rocky land of the south gave way to the fertility of the coast, with its orchards of oranges and bananas and almonds—a pretty town with whitewashed domes and minarets, a coastline with busy, swaggering fishermen. My mother had not even ventured to Sidon when she made the decision to move to Beirut. But it was a passage of necessity.

Before she left, as she was to tell my brother in the years to come, a maternal uncle of my father, one of the "big men" of our small world, a feared colonel in the gendarmes, had come by and asked her to stick around. He said that he would take care of her and her children, that his Beiruti wife would not have to know anything about it, that he would keep it a secret from his sister and my grandmother, the feared Rawshna. Secrets in Arnoun: my mother was too shrewd to believe in such things. Two divorces had broken her back, but this slide downward into dishonor was an entirely different thing. She knew that it would spell ruin for her sons, that they would be outcast. Nothing would have been handier for the husband who had discarded her: a trip to the bed of Najib Bey, the old colonel with white skin and blue eyes and an effeminate lisp, would have been an easy warrant for my father to wash his hands clean of any responsibility for us. The wrath of my grandfather, the patriarch of the family, would have known no limits. There had always been a running feud between

my grandfather and the brothers of his wife, those white-skinned Alawiyya men and government officials, sons of a man who had by one stratagem or another dispossessed my grandfather of part of his inheritance. My mother—divorced, discarded—was still part of my grandfather's clan. She was his daughter-in-law, and she was the mother of his two oldest grandchildren, both males.

My mother came to the city with a promise from my grandfather that there would be enough help for her in Beirut, that he would make that "wretched son" of his give a few liras every month to keep a roof over our heads. She knew the ways of the world; she knew the dangers: "Away from the eyes, away from the heart," she said.

Arnoun was behind her and behind us. Only my grandparents remained in Arnoun. They were the last of us to whom the land was whole, to whom it gave both identity and material means. They neither loved nor hated it. They knew how many acres of land they had—*dunams* to be more precise. They knew the rhythm of the seasons. They knew when tobacco had to be planted, when it had to be brought from the field to the shed, and when the dreaded inspectors of the Régie showed up. Wheat was sown and then harvested; tobacco could never be taken for granted. It required ceaseless labor and attention throughout the year, from the time the seed was put into the ground until the inspectors showed up to price it and weigh it and haul it off to the Régie's factories in Beirut. My grandmother knew how many eggs her hens laid. Woe to the peasant hands who thought that Sitt Rawshna was too busy to notice such things. My grandparents' small orchard of fig trees stood on top of a hill just before the final climb to Beaufort. It was a "piece of land" that my grandmother had brought into her marriage, and it was an orchard she favored. From the roof of her house in the center of Arnoun, my

grandmother could see, and could bring to account, those fool-hardy enough to raid the figs of Shaykh Muhammad's household.

For the rest of us—the second generation of unmarried un-cles and aunts, my father with his second wife and new children, my brother and I—Arnoun lay in the past. But the village would continue to beckon. We drew from that land our identity. We were *from* Arnoun. We would be *from* it no matter how far we traveled. Our country classified things with finality. The identity cards issued by our government specified Arnoun as birthplace and as home and as voting domicile. Arnoun was hard to shake off. "Oh, there goes Fouad, grandson of Shaykh Muhammad from Arnoun."

My father and my uncles and aunts, the sons and daughters of Shaykh Muhammad and Rawshna, must have anticipated the coming exile from the land. They themselves had been given clearly Shia names—Ali, Abbas, Hussein for the men; Sakna, Zaynab, Sakiba for the women. These were names that came from behind a line. These were Shiite names. But the names of the third generation—my older brother's, mine, those of younger cousins and brothers and sisters—were different. We were sent into the world with "borderline" names. Fouad could be the name of a Christian or a Sunni or a Druze. It was a name for the city, given to see me through, I presume, without sirens, without lights flash-ing and giving away my origins and my sect. My father, who gave me the name, must have wanted me to walk undetected in the world of strangers. There had to be, in my family, promptings of a world beyond the land and the immemorial ways. I had not at-tributed those kinds of yearnings to them when I was growing up.

Arnoun was our summer home. We all said how we loved the land, how we ached to be there, to hear the crickets chirping away, to clear the thistles from the vineyard, to go and sleep under the

weary fig trees, to watch the peasant women in the tobacco shed stacking the leaves of tobacco before they lanced iron skewers through the stem, pulled them onto threads to make garlands, and put them out to be dried by the sun. We all remembered the cool water of the Litani River, the delight of jumping into it after surviving the treacherous downward scramble from the rocks of Arnoun. We treasured the memories of springtime in our village. The hills, barren throughout the year, suddenly knee-deep with wild flowers and scented thyme, the lilies that somehow managed to find red patches of earth among the rocks.

We still had in us the inherited ways of the land. We claimed that we could go back, and in faraway places we praised the land. But the land to our back would no longer sustain or feed us. We were being banished from the ungiving land.

But the people who stayed on the land, who were its trustees and spokesmen, insisted that it was the measure of all things, that it was bigger than the comings and goings of men. It was said there that the land anchored everyone. A parliamentary seat could be won and lost, it was said. A thriving business in Saudi Arabia could come to an end if one cut a corner too many or angered one of the thousand and one princes in that country. Achievement in Africa could be blown away if a soldier came to power and thought the Lebanese traders should be undone. The fortunes of men were transient affairs, it was declared by the keepers of the land. The world outside was unpredictable. Only the land was secure and complete.

Sons and daughters went to Beirut and then, when Beirut would not accommodate them, to the far ends of the earth. Grandsons acquired the new skills and the new education of the modern world. But they were, supposedly, to remain faithful to the phobias and to the prohibitions of the land. The land

and those on it were complete and unshaken. It was the banished progeny that had to prove itself and to return for periodic judgments.

Success had to come and pay homage, to be certified as it were, in the house of Shaykh Muhammad and Rawshna. And in the house of stone with street-level windows, there was no trace of insecurity. Children and grandchildren battled garlands of tobacco for space, and swallows nested in the corners of the ceilings. On one side of the house was a ruined old barn where Arnounis came and defecated. On the other was a dung heap that overlooked a particularly stubborn piece of land whose tobacco plants were always more stunted, more hesitant, than the plants in other fields. But the house of the Shaykh, secure behind its iron gate, which was there only for reasons of self-respect and status, rendered its judgment with a cool kind of indifference on the errands of the restless progeny. The house acknowledged the comings and goings, took in the grief and the heartbreak along with the bits of triumph. We knew that only the successful dared return to have their new skills and their trophies and achievements receive the blessing of silent and stern souls. Instilled in each of us was the unspoken fear that one might indeed return there a failure, imprisoned by the land and by the watchful eyes.

A young man entered the realm of manhood when he came on his own into Grandmother Rawshna's domain and brought with him what his father always brought when he returned. Her entourage of old women, bent and diminished by the years, women with one foot in the grave, women who were once handy around the house but were now kept around out of sympathy and habit and obligation, always joined her in her prayer and good wishes. They hoped that there was enough for the wife of the shaykh to be generous. They knew that it would be hard for her

to cut them out of what the Almighty had provided. They knew that the lady herself had to think about meeting her creator in due time and had to worry about the day of judgment and resurrection. Surely she knew better than to meet God and his imams without earning the merit that came from handing old Amsha, now nearly blind, some of what the young man had brought. Wily Amsha was no fool. She knew all the lady's sons and daughters and grandsons by name. She could recall how everyone had, some years ago, worried about the young man's deeds, wrote him off for his recurrent troubles at school. But God, bigger and mightier than the ill-wishers, had answered the prayer: the demon within the young man had been stilled. Amsha knew that an additional prayer for a son of the shaykh who had not written from Liberia for some time would cut off the lady's routes of escape. On this day, Amsha and the other old women in Sitt Rawshna's circle would leave the shaykh's house with some of the things that money earned in faraway places had brought back to the land and the people who remained on the land.

—⁂—

We were not the only ones to leave the land of Arnoun, but we were the first. Others were to follow. In the summer, in the threshing fields on the outskirts of the village, heaps of golden-yellow wheat that shimmered in the sun were circled by the oxen that ground down the bushels of grain, leaving mounds of chaff, one right close to the other. But now the threshing fields were becoming a thing of the past.

Rashid Mousa's plough could no longer make a straight furrow in his plot of land; his mind trailed from his work and the furrow meandered through the soil. A man of some means, who

knew his way around the government ministries, promised him a job in the city as a cable-car operator. The plough was set aside, and the sturdy peasant made his way to the outskirts of Beirut on the running board of Haidar's Model T.

The one day when Haidar had run his car down, having taken it as far as it could be taken, he left what remained of it in front of his home and headed off to the oil fields of Saudi Arabia to make his fortune.

II

In Beirut, I shuttled between the one-story house that my father had built for himself and his new family and the room with the tin roof that my mother had rented for herself, halfway between my father's house and the school that he had built, called the National School. The house, the room with the tin roof, and the school were in Bourj Hammoud, an Armenian squatter settlement on the outskirts of Beirut.

I grew up somewhere between my father's capricious triumph and my mother's laments. He hid his weakness and exaggerated his might. She lived by narrating and going over the tales of hurt. He held up an example of merciless triumph. She presented a spectacle of virtuous defeat. He asked for fear and obedience—as much of it as the soul could bear without shriveling in terror. She asked for sympathy—as much of it as the heart could offer yet still be left with shreds for other loves and sorrows.

He wore a tie, and, in time, when some money came his way, he got for himself a pair of sunglasses and a well-tailored suit.

She wore a headscarf and she ran the endless errands she had to do in a pair of wooden clogs. He had his school license, his elementary school, and a house next to a swamp by the railroad tracks. She arrived in Beirut with her mattress, utensils, and Singer sewing machine. Her clothes were wrapped the peasant way—in a white bundle.

He willed himself into the "modern world" of Beirut and business and foreign travel. She remained who she was and where she was from: a divorced woman, a Shia woman from the south. My mother had a general idea of how old she was. She told me that she was "in her forties" when she was two years short of her fortieth birthday. I had to learn her exact age from her national identification card issued by the Lebanese government. All she knew about the date of her birth was what had been transmitted to her: that the date was sometime around the winter of 1911, when snow and hail had fallen without interruption for thirty-five days. My father, on the other hand, always made an issue of his age: he was precise about it, and he always under-estimated it. He was born in the year 1919, but he said that there had been an error, that he was born in the year 1921. But he had too many brothers and sisters close to him in age for him to get away with his story.

She taught the wisdom of patient defeat: another day, another dawn. She dipped into a vast well of tales, tales as old as the hills, peasant sayings, tales from our rich Shiite heritage. She told the tales in her own way—part consolation, part fatalism, part inducement to go on. "The mule intends one thing, the muleteer intends another, but God's intentions take precedence over all other intentions." This was a saying for the unknown, a way of consoling oneself while facing "muleteers" with all kinds of sordid intentions. He had no need and no time for the tales. He taught a straight lesson of his own: men take what they can.

"Every man pulls his own thorns with his own hands." This, his favorite peasant saying, was what he left the land with.

She was an unlettered woman. The two forms she kept in her possession had her thumb-print: her birth certificate and a deed to a piece of land in her town that she had held onto and hid from her second husband. She stood in awe of those who could make out letters and pitied people like herself who had been denied that kind of power. He exaggerated the few years of schooling that he had had in the town of Nabatiyya. He walked around in the Armenian squatter settlement that became our home—strutted would be a better way of describing his walk, head turned upward—with a newspaper under his arm. The newspaper advertised him to his neighbors as a literate man and a man who cared about the world. It was part of his distinction. He had plans for more education for himself. And, for a while, he enrolled in a night course at one of the city's secondary schools.

He came to the city with the prerogatives of men. He was quick to tell his older brother, who was a government schoolteacher deep in the southern hinterland, of his exploits with his first Christian woman. The world, he repeated to his brother, lay at the feet of those men who tried. The woman was not an Umm Ali or Umm Abbas. It was not one of the Shiite names. She was a divorced woman who had to be careful at every turn. She had my brother and me in her life. She could not throw shadows in our way. We had enough to contend with.

In the Armenian squatter settlement that became our home, he was a medium-size fish in a small pond. He presented himself and talked well. He spoke of his own plans for the future—a secondary school for the neighborhood, progress. He walked into what passed for an office of the Armenian *mukhtar*, the mayor

of these alleyways, with forms to be signed. He declared the *mukhtar* his friend.

He had around the house two or three newspaper clippings of articles that he had written in the Communist newspaper, *Al-Tariq*. He had joined the party, and he had broken with it. Both deeds did him honor, he said. He had been alert enough to join. The Communists had talked of equality, of electrification of the countryside, of irrigating the scrub land of the South. They had pointed with great pride to what was being done in the faraway Russian home of Communism; they made much of the valor, of the manhood of Stalin. My father was an alert "son of a bitch." He was alert enough to give the new party a try. But he insisted that he was alert enough to let well enough alone. There was no "bread" in Communism, in its pamphlets, he said. The membership in the party was dropped. He was a man of affairs now—and responsibility. But the memory of the Party and its days of exuberance—and the clippings—remained. He was a man trying, a man leaving no stone unturned.

Another clipping in particular was dearer to his heart than those from the Communist paper. It was a clipping of an article he had written for the *Telegraph*, one of the principal daily newspapers in Beirut. "The Mules of the South Are Better Off than Its People" was the title of the article. It may have been only a letter to the editor, but he took pride in it, held onto it through the years. Its subject was the timeless one of our region's poverty and backwardness. The mules, he wrote, would have rebelled against the conditions of the South. But the people of the South continued to endure the ills of "feudalism" and oppression. He was an articulate son of the South putting forward the grievances of the South in a paper of the city. The piece from the *Telegraph* was yellowed but well preserved. (Years later, in 1958, when the

owner of the *Telegraph* was murdered, his loss was seen as something personal.)

He was the "first" in his family to flirt with such political ideas, the "first" to come and knock at the gates of a bigger world. My mother had no great claims.

Way beyond the world that he lived and operated in were men mightier than my father, men with real power, men with wealth, with a margin for error. There was a Beiruti politician with an ever-fresh carnation in his lapel who was always prime minister or candidate for the post. There was a corpulent Druze "prince" with a waxed moustache turned upward at the tips who was always defense minister ("Minister of Bom-Bom" was the way the wisecracks described him) and who married one of the country's ravishing beauties. There was a politician with a red fez who either had the job of speaker of parliament or was beaten for the job by his son-in-law. There was a finicky and precocious man whose first name was Henry and whose last name translated into "Pharaoh" who owned tens and tens of beautiful race horses and a famed collection of Chinese and Islamic art. There were men who smiled from the pages of newspapers and magazines, drinks in hand with glamorous, heavily made-up women next to them, celebrating what life gave them. There was a man who had a table of his own at the Hotel Saint Georges. The fawning journalists covered the comings and goings of those who were invited to join him at his table. There was a man, presumably a Lebanese like the rest of us, who called himself Marquis De Freij and never bothered to explain to mere mortals where his title came from or what it meant.

There was a newspaper publisher, old and corpulent, who, with the help of a variety of embassies and political patrons, built for himself three publications: a magazine whose name translated

to *The Fisherman*, a gossip magazine named *The Net*, and a newspaper named *The Lights*. Each week, in a column in one of his magazines, the corpulent man told of his sexual exploits in Beirut and in faraway cities, of beautiful young women who submitted to him. He told of the gifts given to him by men in power.

There were men and women whom the foreign visitors to our country met. It was with tales about them, tales of an exquisite and polished people who lived on the shores of the Mediterranean, that they returned home. But my father didn't know these men, nor did my mother. The world was what was known to them. And in that world he had claims and pretensions. Her story was written, her life behind her.

—m—

I was to live with my mother in the room with the tin roof and go to the National School with the four rooms, overflowing latrines, and a dark and narrow and long space that was the office of my father, the school's principal and owner. This had been decreed by my grandfather.

But things were never settled. There were times when he didn't want to pay the liras promised her, times when my brother and I were pulled out of the classroom and told to go get our stuff and take it to my father's and step-mother's house by the swamp. But more than money was at stake in those sudden bursts of temper. In part, it was his fight with the wife of his past, his rage at her. We were not needed or appreciated in the house by the swamp. But denying us to my mother was part of his retribution, of his way of exercising his power over her. He had come to this new place amidst new people. She had trailed him here. Were we to remain with him, she would be left in the city without a

mission, without an identity. Questions would then arise as to what a divorced woman was doing on her own in the city. In his own way, he continued to think of her as a piece of the past, of the tucked-away villages of the South. He would have loved to see her swallowed by the earth, but he would have settled for her return to the town she had left behind.

The house by the swamp, the house my father had built, was a veritable obsession of my mother's. It was a testimony to the womanly powers of my step-mother, the younger woman. Women lived through men: they sent them on errands and stayed at home. A lucky woman, it was said, walked from the home of her father to that of her husband. This was the highest ambition: a life lived as it should be. A woman was supposed to endure the cruelty, the nature, the *tabia'a*, of a man, to find a way around his caprice, to hold off the challenges of other women.

There was no shortage of good souls who paid a visit to the house by the swamp and reported back to my mother on what they saw. The good souls always made the house grand and tranquil, a place of triumph. Word had come that a brand-new Frigidaire had been added to the *dar* of Ali Ajami, that the lady of the house didn't have to lift a finger at home, that the daughter of a tenant in the house did the household chores. The bearers of the news were thanked for the keen eye they had for what they had seen: "Yes, my dear Umm Abdu, I know that Khadija has the place that should have been mine. And I do know that Ali Ajami is quite a man among men, that he has the walk and bearing of men. And how could I not know? I was married to the man, in accord with the law of God and his Prophet. He is the father of my two sons. He can go to the far ends of the earth. And then one day, they will be there to bury and inherit him. My dear friend, don't concern yourself with what goes on in the *dar* of Ali Ajami."

The God-fearing souls here loved to remind others of their failures. There was really no place to hide, no chance for a wound to heal. Ahmad, the cross-eyed man, was called Ahmad *al Ahwal*, Ahmad the cross-eyed. Adnan, born with a deformity in his leg that left him unable to walk like others, was always identified by his deformity. There goes Adnan *al Kassiha*, Adnan the cripple. An argument with a divorced woman was brought to a quick end when *al Mutallaqa*, the divorced one, was reminded that surely had she had something to offer or to say—something worth listening to—the Almighty would have left her a lady in her own domain under a husband's roof. No scab was left on a wound. No violation was ever forgotten. The house by the swamp was a steady reminder of the spell of one woman, of the defeat of another.

I identified the house by the swamp with and through Abu Khasba, the man with the wooden leg and hard, craven face who rented a room in my father's house. Abu Khasba (literally meaning father of wood, the man with the wood) was the name I had given him, the name my mother had thrown at him when she asked him to mind his own filthy business and to know his limits. Abu Khasba had loved to call my father by the name of his eldest son born to my step-mother. By tradition, a father went by the name of his eldest son. Thus my father was to be Abu Riad, Riad's father. But Abu Khasba was "with he who was up." Nothing personal. It was just that Abu Khasba loved a winner, and he knew what side to be on. In his household, sympathy with winners was a wish that someday some triumph would come their way. No gains came his way when he called my father Abu Issam, or Issam's father. But the name was a great affront to my mother, to the claims of her two sons. When my mother crossed paths with Abu Khasba, she gave him an exquisite piece of her oratory: God

knew what to do with him. He had taken away his leg. My mother prophesied more misfortune for Abu Khasba.

Abu Khasba loved a story. He offered it to those who asked for it and those who didn't, when it fit and when it didn't. It was a story about the folly of teaching archery that he attributed to our venerable Imam Ali, the first imam. "So soon as the arm of the archer becomes steady," Abu Khasba said, "the teacher will be the archer's first victim." There was no gratitude in the world, Abu Khasba pronounced: Bani Adam, sons of Adam, bit the hand that fed them and went their own way. "Take the two boys, Riad and Fouad. They receive every break in the *dar*, in the house of Ali Ajami and Lady Khadija, but they will forget."

I shivered in the cold on my way to school, in a black cotton frock that was called a school uniform. I was trying to make my way through the hellish Arabic grammar, to avoid the physical beatings that came when mistakes were made. But Abu Khasba was worried about my skills in archery.

The birds in the house by the swamp, I was told, saw me drop by my mother's place on my way to school. The birds reported that I was given a hearty meal on my way to school by my mother, who was supposed to stay away and who was breaking the rules. Abu Khasba's daughter, a girl with a turned-up nose and a bossy manner, ten or eleven years old when I was about six, saw me meander on my way to school.

Ustadh Ibrahim, Teacher Ibrahim, was one of the gentle folk enlisted by my mother whenever she ran afoul of my father's instructions. Ustadh Ibrahim was a kindly man, a simple villager coughed up by the countryside. He was the all-purpose man at the National School—vice principal, teacher of grammar, accountant—and he had the concessions to sell seeds and nuts and cotton candy during lunch hours and breaks. The ways of the

village burst through the worn-out suit, the only one that Teacher Ibrahim had. He himself was the victim of my father's harangues and capricious ways. Tall and emaciated, Teacher Ibrahim recognized himself in the divorced woman slipping food to her children, seeing them only when it was safe to do so. Teacher Ibrahim knew the comings and goings of his employer. An excursion by my father to the home of Umm Tony was enough time for me to make it to my mother's place and then return to school. An excursion to the home of Umm Ahmad, the vital and dark Palestinian woman, was a risky affair. These were shorter: the deed done, the owner of the school returned in no time.

Abu Khalil, a pillar of this neighborhood, one of its "big men," was another man my mother petitioned in her constant struggle to keep us with her. Abu Khalil was also from the South. He was a friend of my father's father, slightly younger than the patriarch of Arnoun. The webs of the old world meant a great deal to Abu Khalil. He remembered the days of his youth when he had gone to Khiam: the fellowship he had known there, the elaborate meals, the passionate weddings, the great funerals, the town poets reciting their poems until the early hours of dawn. Abu Khalil was married to three women. He prided himself on his fairness to all three of them. He wanted other men to be fair. His first wife had been the wife of his youth, of his early battles: she was the mother of his sons. His second wife was a decade younger than the first wife. Then there was his youngest wife, the almond-eyed young widow who had come to Abu Khalil seeking help with the municipality over some matter or another. Abu Khalil, normally a man of poise and quiet strength, was smitten by the young widow. He had not planned a third marriage; his sons had fought with him over this plan. He knew he could have had his way with the young widow, that he could have kept her as

a mistress as his sons had suggested. But he was a stubborn man, Abu Khalil, and was not to be dissuaded. He wanted a marriage in accord with the law of God and His Prophet, and he was sure he could dispense justice to all of his wives. He rotated his days among the three and prided himself on his fairness. He wanted other men to be as fair as he knew he was.

If and when the periods at the house by the swamp got unduly long, and Abu Khalil's interventions failed, word was sent by my mother to the patriarch in Arnoun, my grandfather.

Shaykh Muhammad came unannounced. There was a way that messages could be sent to the alleyway through drivers and passengers coming from the town of Nabatiyya. But my grandfather preferred his sudden visits. Abu Khasba squirmed when the old man showed up: he addressed my father by the name of his eldest son. And he dropped out of sight.

My grandfather came bearing the gifts of Arnoun—a bucket of fresh yogurt, a basket of figs, some eggs, some *burghul*, bulgur wheat. He came in his white *kafiyya*, with his *abaya*, gown, over his shoulders and his cane in his hand—a tall and erect man free of any self-consciousness and doubts. Others of the countryside may have felt squeamish about their attire and identity in this city that was so nervous about the "primitive," the rural, the past. But my grandfather was who he was. He came to call on his son, to look after his grandsons, to check in on his daughters who were living in another part of Beirut with their brothers, my older uncle, Ahmad, and my younger uncle, Abbas.

The shaykh with few words came to visit and to see. He had objections, he said, to boys being raised by women. But it was clear to him that things in Ali's home were not the way they should be. It was not the shaykh's problem when Ali divorced the first wife and opted for the second. But the two boys were

the shaykh's problem. The two boys had the shaykh's name and blood. Yes, he had doubts about boys raised by women. But under the circumstances—the sweaters on the children from the second marriage, the light cotton frocks on children from the first—the shaykh was not ready to say that boys should not be raised by a mother.

When our presence in his house seemed to disrupt the routine of his life with his wife and new children, Ali Ajami would, like a sultan, announce that we were on our way to stay with my mother. Then he would change his mind: the change would be triggered by her request—always through intermediaries to whom he always appeared entirely reasonable—for some money. The rage came later, always after the intermediaries had left. Then we would be back in his home, in the house by the swamp and the railroad tracks; then we would again be in his presence—his brooding watchfulness, his outbursts of temper, and always his angry eyes. We were clearly in his way. But unseen to two bewildered children, my father was battling the odds. The debts—*fatateer*, IOU notes—began to accumulate.

Once or twice, my grandfather threatened to take me and my brother back to the village. We could be schooled in Nabatiyya, he said. There was the school run by nuns in *Harat al Nasara* where my older brother and two or three of my aunts had gone before. They had talked of the place with some fondness. They remembered the kindness of the nuns. But my aunts and my brother had complained of the difficult walk on the unpaved road between Arnoun and Nabatiyya.

In my mind the village had left one vivid memory that made me recoil at the idea of a return to Nabatiyya and Arnoun: it was the memory of one harsh winter, our last there. Snow had fallen on the ridge, covered Beaufort Castle, dusted the hills. The wind

came howling, whistling through the treetops. Arnoun's homes were either vulnerable hovels or houses of stone, cold shiny stone, built for the warm summer. No one in Arnoun, not even Shaykh Muhammad's household, had been ready for that winter's assault.

A Syrian garrison was stationed at Beaufort that winter—a remnant of the fight in 1948 between Arab and Jew in Palestine. The war had ended in defeat for the Syrians and the other Arab armies, but the Syrians had kept an observation post at Beaufort. The Syrian soldiers were the only ones around who had appropriate winter attire—heavy khaki coats, sturdy boots. They also had supplies of bread, fat loaves that they distributed to the villagers. I remembered the winter, the villagers scrambling for bread. Decorum was maintained in my grandfather's household. Grandmother Rawshna prided herself on her "open hand" generosity. Some years back, she was keen to remind everyone, loads of people from Khiam, some thirty to forty relatives of my grandfather, had been driven out of their own homes by the fighting between the Free French and the armies of Vichy. The Khiamis had sought shelter in Arnoun. They had been fed and cared for, as honored guests should be. She had always run a good home. Rawshna Alawiyya's provisions always had a way of materializing when they were needed, right when everyone had hinted that the household of Shaykh Muhammad was about to run out of flour and wheat or that the supplies of lentils and the sugar bought from Nabatiyya had been exhausted. No one in our household scrambled for the bread. But we suffered the winter and the biting cold.

The winters in our alleyway were the warmest on the Mediterranean coast. At times, heavy rains fell, which carried away the red earth, overtaxed the sewers of the neighborhood, flooded street-level rooms. Roofs of tin shacks were blown away

by the wind. I could wade through the water in our alleyways in a pair of rubber boots that my mother had bought for me from Bata stores. Orange peelings floated on puddles, raced down newly formed streams, swirled past drainage holes before they were finally swallowed up. Invariably, there was always the sun, storming back, burning through the clouds—the peace of a world resuming its routine.

It wasn't just the easier winter of Beirut that made me cling to the new place with wild-eyed devotion. There were the sounds of the city and the alleyways, radios blasting away with abandon. The songs of Kawkab al Sharq, the star of the East, of the celebrated Egyptian Umm Kulthum, of Farid al Atrash, the crooner known as the "sad sparrow" floated through the streets. I still remember the stern silence of Arnoun. The battery-operated radio in my grandfather's home, the sole radio in the village, was saved for the daily reading of the Quran. During Ramadan, the Muslim month of fasting, we listened for the sunset gun that brought the day of fasting to an end: the sunset gun fired off, that was the end of the radio for the day. The battery was heavy and expensive, and it had to be bought in Nabatiyya. And besides, music was *bida'a*, innovation—something flighty and subversive. The words of flippant, provocative love songs were out of place in the hemmed-in, sober world of the village. A great-uncle of mine, one of the Alawiyya brothers, had an old-fashioned gramophone. Years ago, his father had given him a choice of a gift: a trip to Istanbul or a gramophone. He had chosen his beloved gramophone. It was an item of prestige, proof of his own distinctiveness, that he played for his friends on special occasions. Boys could go and sit outside on the steps of his house and listen to the music. But the whole thing was frowned upon. And the uncle had always been regarded as a bit "odd," not quite "the man" he should have been.

One haircut in the city made it possible for a boy to see the atrocity of his old-country haircut. Ali Qassim, who doubled up as the village's butcher, cut hair in Arnoun. But the first visit to the barber in the alleyways flattered a child. The barber was a dandy, and he took pride in his work. He did it with skill and grace in front of a mirror, and he was generous with the water and the perfume he sprayed on the boy's hair. The work done, he made sure to part it in a flattering way on the side—the way of the city.

Our village was an austere place. The work of the land never ceased. It had been easy to keep track of us all, the children of the village, in an exposed hamlet with so few trees. A sun-charred peasant who worked for my grandfather doubled up as his "public crier." From the roof of the low house in the center of the village, Hussein Hanoun, with his booming voice, summoned other peasants and the grandchildren idling the day away in the fields and among the rocks of Arnoun to come and report to Shaykh Muhammad. So commanding was Hussein's voice that it bounced back off the rocks beyond the village and the ruined walls of Beaufort Castle. The city, with its alleyways and its tumult, offered a great escape from the restrictions of that austere village life. Mahmud Aqeel, a wise man from Arnoun, said of the city that it was a place without masters. Dama, poor Dama, an older distant cousin of mine, jumped to her death from a Beirut balcony rather than go back to the village. The eerie silence of the village and the rocks, she was to say shortly before she leapt to her death, were an unbearable source of terror to her.

My mother had "named" my father's village. She had turned it into a place of cruelty and misfortune. She had given that unpaved road that connected Arnoun to the rest of the world her sense of bitterness and defeat. She had walked to the *wa'ar*, to the wilderness beyond Arnoun. And in those vivid stories of Arnoun,

the place and the harsh wilderness merged. Our village opened onto the town of Nabatiyya, found its way to the outer world through that town. But that town, too, had been named. It was in that larger, more pretentious town that my father had found a new life. And it was from that town that he returned to Arnoun now and then to bicker with his father over the children from the first marriage, to complain that he was a mere "boy" when the two children came along, to plead and shout and no doubt get red in the face over the older man's insistence that he, Ali, had a responsibility for his marriage and to the two children who were born to that marriage.

Defeat invited shame into our world. Defeat sought to encircle, to close in the world of its victim. It set out to erect boundaries beyond which the defeated shouldn't have bothered dreaming of venturing. Our story in the village was known. It trailed us like a shadow. I was a grandchild of Shaykh Muhammad: this gave me some footing in the rural world into which I was born. But it brought with it only exposure and expectations. I was and remained a discarded child of a discarded marriage.

The alleyways of the ghetto into which I had come jumbled my story with that of others. I grew to treasure the anonymity of the place: the village was becoming a memory. I was becoming a child of the alleyways, of the streets—a city slicker. Not so long after my arrival, my pleadings and guile worked to convince my mother to buy me a bright blue water pistol that I treasured. The children of Arnoun played with the bones of dead animals for toys. For a child at once curious and anxious to escape what he knew at home, the new sights, and the new tastes, of the city held their own wonder. An Armenian man in the alleyways sold something called *Fresca*: crushed ice with fruit-syrup. A boy from the country, I saw the multitude of colors in the bottles lined up

by the Armenian as the colors of the city. A cotton-candy vendor wheeled his cart past my school. He had to be a magician: the stuff, circles of pink and circles of white, formed on the sides of a revolving wheel in the middle of his cart. The *mortadella* sandwich, bought for the first time from a Christian shopkeeper—that, too, was a gift of the city. The glamor of the foreign word, the experience of the taste. My mother's panic that the *mortadella* must surely be the dreaded meat of the *khanzir*, the pig, must have been part of the thrill of it all.

There were still patches of wilderness when my family came to settle in Bourj Hammoud. At dawn my brother and I, dispatched to get milk for my father's household from an Armenian seller of milk, stepped into a dark void. But in no time, the swamps were cleared, and the orange orchards and strawberry fields gave way to rows of cinder-block housing. The Armenians who had preceded us here by three decades were leaving the tin shacks behind for one- or two-story cement houses. Almost overnight, it seemed, the daily walks to school that were made through empty spaces had to be made through crowded alleyways: past busy hawkers and new shops; past men in a hurry to make it to the cable-car stop at the outer edge of the neighborhood that carried them to their shops and factories in the center of the city; past butchers setting carcasses of meat out on iron hooks to be admired by those who could afford meat and those who couldn't; past "factory girls" braving their way to work, stashing their headscarves forced on them by their elders into their lunch bags.

Whole villages in the impoverished southern part of the country and in the more backward Bekaa Valley in the eastern

part, close to Syria, were being deserted. Their people were appearing in our settlement. Each village brought its distinct twang. The place spoke in a tumult of dialects and intonations.

It was easy to spot new claimants to the city. There was a clumsiness that gave them away, a certain reverence in the way they shook hands with and greeted others, a certain hesitancy in the way they took to the streets. There was the color of the country, the gift of labor in the fields.

Then the city did its miracle. The peasant coloring disappeared. A young man who only yesterday was a peasant to his fingertips turned up with a new way of combing his hair—pompadour style, of course. And the hair, now greased with a handful of Brylcreem, gathered the dust of the city, of the workshops. Another, newly arrived from the village, landed a job as a cable car operator. He became breezier and more cavalier in the way he encountered other men. Hitherto, he had the peasant way of greeting. Hitherto, the simple query dragged on in endless variations: "How are you? How have you been faring? How is the health of your beloved ones? Allah willing, I hope all is well, that you never know a sad day, that we are never deprived of your care. How are you?…" Now he barely acknowledged those he greeted.

Another boy suddenly showed up with a new watch. It was the same boy who yesterday was seen being dragged by the ear by his stern father to be delivered to the shop of an Armenian master at shoemaking. The father had authorized the Armenian to be merciless toward the boy, to treat him as though he was "one of his own." Now the apprentice shoemaker kept time for himself and for others, for those who asked and for those who didn't. The boy was teased about the watch. He was teased for days. Then the watch became "his" and the episode was forgotten.

A neighbor from the Bekaa Valley, Abu Hamza, who had arrived as penniless as the others, hit it lucky. He won twenty-five thousand pounds in the lottery: he bought a bus, which he ran between the center of Beirut and our neighborhood, put on airs, became a local celebrity. The good luck in the city bore out the man's belief that the Almighty never put a single soul on this earth without having a scheme for him or for her.

A young woman who only yesterday had landed a job in a tobacco factory, and who no doubt was the first woman in her family to venture into the world outside her family's cocoon, dropped her *tarba*, headscarf, for a skimpier, more flamboyant scarf. Then, lo and behold, the scarf disappeared, and the young woman insisted that she had all along appeared in public without a scarf.

We shared these alleyways with men and women from a different world. There were lines. But the lines broke down, the lines crossed and ran into the small worlds of other men and women and children. There were Christians. But more exotically, more vividly for me, we had moved into an Armenian world.

Most of the Armenians had preceded us here by a good quarter-century. The place had begun as a refugee camp, set up by the League of Nations. Women and children had marched in convoys through the Syrian Desert to this settlement here. They had come here in the aftermath of the terrible calamities inflicted on them by the Turks in the years of the Great War and the great famine that devastated our land. They had come bearing their sorrows and their dreams of a time when the world would be put right again, and they would find their way back to Armenia. They thought of themselves as a "nation in temporary exile." More than a hundred thousand Armenians were living in Lebanon by the late 1940s. The majority must have been our neighbors.

I didn't know a great deal about the Armenians. At dawn, on those errands we ran to fetch milk for my father's household, my brother and I had an agreement that we should always greet the Armenians we ran into by saying *"Marhaba, Khawaja,"* "Hello, sir." We feared the Armenians. Or, more likely, we thought we should. The Armenians were drinkers, it was said by the Shiite squatters. But in truth, the Armenians were a hardworking, energetic breed. They were skilled artisans and mechanics. They turned this settlement into a beehive of activity. The small crafts, the workshops were all Armenian endeavors. An Armenian home for the blind was on the way to my school. Many a morning, I would stop to watch men and women stringing together chairs of straw. My people tormented the blind and the elderly: children chased them down streets, heckled them, reminded them of their lot. The Armenians cared for their own.

The fine differences among the Armenians eluded us. They had come here in waves. Some were exiled after grim massacres at the hands of the Ottoman Sultan Abdul Hamid in the 1890s. Others were victims of the "enlightened" Young Turks who overthrew the Ottoman order and promised everyone a bright new world, only to massacre even larger numbers of Armenians during the years of the famine and the Great War. A few wandered here in the late 1930s, ten years before my family had come.

The cruelties of the world, the sordid diplomatic game between Russia and Turkey, had thrown together proud mountaineers from Armenia and polished city folk and artisans from Constantinople, peasants and merchants, the fanatically religious and the emancipated socialist. A line ran through their world, dividing Hunchaks, who identified themselves with the Armenian Soviet Socialist Republic, and Dashnaks, who were fervent anti-Communists. The Hunchaks were compulsive pamphleteers.

71

The young men who were busy at daybreak slipping their pamphlets under the doors of the shopkeepers went about their task with zeal and enthusiasm. The pamphleteers had causes in ample supply: they protested visits to our shores by the US Sixth Fleet; they spoke of distant causes in Korea and China, of the follies of Anglo-American imperialism, of the greed of oil companies laying down pipelines through our country, of social security for the poor. These were men who had been awakened and mobilized by larger causes, who had been given public politics.

All I knew of the Hunchaks and Dashnaks was that they fielded two formidable rival soccer teams: the Homannen and the Homenetmen. My favorite player, Mardik, with the crew cut and the exquisitely placed shots, played for the Hunchak team. "*Marhaba, Mardik*," "Hello, Mardik," I said. He must have been about twenty years old then, a good decade older than his enthralled fan. After looking me over for what seemed like an eternity, Mardik, charitable that day, acknowledged my presence. I floated on dreams for the rest of the day, had fantasies of a brilliant soccer future of my own.

The Armenians had said that they were here for only a brief time. But they stayed. This became the second Armenia. Here in these alleyways, the Armenian passion played itself out. The refugees brought with them the names of their old towns and villages and assigned them to these crooked streets and quarters. New Sis, New Adana, New Marsh, New Hajn. Three different churches claimed the loyalty of the Armenians. There were Catholic Armenians and Protestant Armenians, but the majority were adherents of the Apostolic Armenian Church. Some Armenians read the newspaper *Ararat*; others were devoted readers of *Azdak*. Some voted in elections for a wealthy Armenian journalist by the name of Tigran Tospat, a perennial candidate

for Parliament. Some loathed Tospat because he had converted from the Armenian Catholic Church to the Apostolic Armenian Church. Tospat's politics were beyond me. I loved his name though. I knew his name by the way it was written on banners and posters in Arabic script: Dikran Tospat. Tospat was capable of great flip-flops: he could be for the government or against it. He could be the Dashnak candidate, or he could be on the rival list. Some Armenians may have loathed him as an opportunist. I was fixated on his name—a child's fixation on something melodic and unfamiliar.

The Armenian passion for the details of the old country, for its sharply drawn lines, was really an act of fidelity to a world and a country that was no more. The names and the cuisine of the old world were brought here with the orphans and the widows.

We lived in proximity to that passion. The Armenians were light years ahead of us. We could not have understood them. There was an Armenian theater group, an Armenian relief society. We had come into their world. There we were cannibalizing one another, hacking away at one another. Each man among us stood in utter, desperate isolation: the medium-size fish devoured the smaller one. Women and children had to fend for themselves. The Armenians took in that entire spectacle. What they said, what they thought of my mother with her wooden clogs and her headscarf, of my father with his newspaper under his arm, of the students at the National School with their black cotton frocks chanting the Lebanese National Anthem, they kept to themselves.

It must have been a good place, a friendly place for dreams and memories of lost homelands, this neighborhood of ours, the right kind of place for men and women who carried their homelands on their backs. Palestinian refugees who had taken to the road in 1948, under the belief that the valiant Arab armies

would in time put the Jews to flight and restore their old homes and villages, swarmed over our neighborhoods. They, too, like the Armenians, said that they would not be here for long, that this was but a dark interlude in their lives. I was schooled early in this geography of dispossession. There were men of Haifa, I learned, and men of Jaffa: The people of Haifa treasured memories of a time when the prosperous *Ingliz* had built a pipeline from Baghdad to Haifa, turning their city into the envy of Bilad al Sham. The Jaffa people were more poetic about their city. The scent of orange orchards trailed the people of the proud city of Jaffa right to these alleyways, and the pomegranates of their memory grew larger and sweeter with the years of their dispossession. The people said of their city that it was the "gateway to Palestine." Cobblestone streets opened onto a magic harbor where ships from every port of call, ships of every color, carried on Jaffa's trade. The peace of her evenings was broken only by the sound of horse-drawn carriages traversing its streets. Men were playthings in the hands of destiny, the Jaffawis said. One storm and nests could be blown away and scattered into the wind. Streams of cool water ran through the orange orchards of Jaffa's gardens; the sea by the coast crawled and glistened in the sun.

"Two kinds of people you can never trust: the Communists because they don't believe in God and the Palestinians because they have no land." The words were my mother's. She drew her line of empathy close to her own kinsmen, to the sounds and places she knew. My mother had two or three small pieces of land. She had her memories of her town. She went back there every now and then and always returned from her visits serene and upbeat, comforted by the valley of her childhood, by the familiar earth, by the graves of the ancestors. Her father had had enough land

to see him through a dignified old age. Men and women without land were incomplete in her eyes.

My mother had grown up a stone's throw, as my people said, from the land fought over by Jew and Arab. A large cataclysmic deed had taken place. The Jews had secured their state, and the Palestinians had taken to the road. But the passion of nationalism that made the plight of the Palestinians an Arab burden, an Arab truth, was not my mother's. The world ended at a particular point, at the feet, close to the fury and the hurt of particular individuals one knew and feared and loved. What was beyond that point, my mother, and the other women with headscarves and men scurrying off to work, neither knew, nor concerned themselves with. Of the entire drama of Palestine played out across the border from where she lived, my mother had retained her own fragment: my father smuggling guns to Palestine, his imprisonment, and then his quick release. She retained another fragment, which had taken place right after she had arrived, a bewildered peasant woman, to Beirut. Palestinian women had staged a demonstration on the streets of Beirut. They wanted their homes back, a way back to the past. It had been a year since they had crossed the border to Lebanon. Many of them still had the keys to their old homes. But the "temporary" stay had dragged on, and the women had taken to the streets. My mother remembered the occasion less for the politics than for the novelty of it all, the ways of the new city into which the world had hurled her.

—⁓—

"The flesh is yours, the bone ours," said the parents who brought their children to my elementary school. In other words, beat them if you will. Children were like olives, our people said: they

had to be pounded and beaten before they were of any use. The parents who brought their children to the elementary were mostly illiterate. They were determined that their children should do better. They wanted them prepared for the competition. If the National School—and its beatings—had the magic to open the door to something better than the parents knew, so be it. They were ready to pay the small monthly fee, to take it out of the food allowance, to forego the wages that young boys and girls could earn on odd jobs, in small shops and factories. And they were ready to sanction the beatings.

The parents needn't have worried. Beatings and Arabic grammar were the specialty of the school. Arabic grammar was the subject of Teacher Ibrahim. He himself had been schooled in his village, taught reading and the Quran by a local shaykh in return for what little could be spared by way of flour, some eggs, an occasional chicken. Teacher Ibrahim was faithful to what he inherited. He had a cane that he named after a deadly snake. He had the right intonations. On particularly warm afternoons, it was hard to stay awake as Teacher Ibrahim repeated again and again the same words: *Da-ra-ja, A-ra-ja*. Even the hard benches with no back support were no antidote to Teacher Ibrahim's cadence. It never occurred to him to explain what these words meant. Classical written Arabic was a world removed, almost a different language, from colloquial Arabic. We repeated what we were asked to repeat.

Arabic grammar was its own torment: it had its capricious ways. The simple word *walad*, boy, could be *walad* or *waladoo*, or *walada* or *waladi*, depending on what the boy was doing or what was being done to him. The grammar asked no understanding and offered none. Rather like the authority of parents and teachers, it asked to be obeyed and submitted to. Our teachers

were fastidious about Arabic grammar. It was
they knew and we did not. They knew that Arabic gra͟n.
a serious, almost sacred matter. The grammar was essential ͟ɯ
writing letters, for giving speeches, for passing government ex-
aminations. It was the grammar of the ancestors, of the Quran,
of the classical poets, of the men who ruled, of the terrifying
speeches they had given, of the commands they had issued. Some
brave and reckless souls had suggested that the grammar could be
simplified, made more bearable, easier to enter. But the heavens
would have fallen. The grammar had been perfected by genera-
tions of men more worthy than ourselves. The grandeur of our
people was situated in times past: the dead and their works hon-
ored us. It would have been heresy to tamper with what the great
princes and their court poets—and grammarians—had left us.

We were asked to come to the board to conjugate sentences
whose meanings we never understood. The word "conjugate" had
its own weight and terror. The lucky ones raced through the task
as teachers stood by with their canes at the ready. A few lashes
from the cane were an easy punishment. Students were beaten,
kicked, slapped across the face. There were floggings for those
perennially in trouble. We vowed to do better. Nimr Ali Muhsin,
hopeless Nimr Ali Muhsin, notorious for the punishments he
received, begged mercy for the dead in Teacher Ibrahim's family
and promised to do better on yet another day. When his appeal
failed, as it always did, he put on a brave front, winking to his
friends as he took his place among us on the crowded bench.

Teacher Ibrahim's punishments were mild when compared
to those administered by my father. There was something im-
personal, matter-of-fact, almost lethargic about the way Teacher
Ibrahim administered his punishments. He was happy to be a
teacher. All was well with him so long as his monthly salary was

paid, so long as there was enough sugar for his cups of tea. He had no great ambition, no desire to go to distant places.

My father was a restless, angry man. The students at the National School were terrified of him. And my older brother, in particular, was to suffer greatly at my father's hands whenever he showed up at school. My brother could never get right the grammar he had crammed or the arithmetic he had been taught. The sacred Arabic grammar was lost on the endless errands that our father had him run. What my brother knew, what he had retained could never be called forth in the intimidating presence of our father. The punishments he received were merciless; they were punishments that even the teachers in our school, teachers never squeamish about physical cruelty, were taken aback by.

Things were not going well for my father. He was not sleeping. It was becoming harder to make ends meet on his income from the school. Ambition had pushed him into this squatter settlement. This had bought time. But he was again at an impasse. He had four new children, two older ones. Little more than two years after the school was built, both it and the house by the swamp were mortgaged to a loan shark from Nabatiyya. My father became unbearable. He had us coming and going to and from my mother's place. He decreed that we had to read more at night, though we had only our reading primer, that we could only go to bed when he authorized it. Several times, late into the night, he either forgot to give the permission for us to go to bed or just refused to do so.

My grandmother worried about him and came from Arnoun. His suffering became more acute. He started coming up with desperate, small schemes to raise money. One such scheme had him bus the whole school to an outing on the banks of a nearby river. Children had to pay for the trip even as parents quibbled.

It was the principal's contention that a trip to Dog River, *Nahr al Kalb*, to its two vast fountains some four miles above the sea—the Fountain of Honey and the Fountain of Milk—was essential to their education. Legend had it that in the long past ages, a monster of the wolf species was chained by some god or demon at the river's mouth, which, when lashed to fury by the storms, awoke the echoes of far-distant Cyprus with his bark. The encircling hills above the river, too, were the stuff of legend and imagination. These were the hills of Adonis, the shepherd-god. Fought over by Aphrodite, queen of the light, and Persephone, queen of the shadows, Adonis was ordered by Zeus to live half the year in the world of light, the other half in the world of shadows. In the surrounding hills, the legend had it that Aphrodite's husband, Ares, god of war, turned himself into a wild boar and killed Adonis. Every year hence, the shepherd's blood and the goddess's tears watered the hills, and Adonis returned to the world of the living. The hills, wild with crimson anemone, celebrated his resurrection. To see the monasteries nestled in those hills, the flowers in bloom, the terraces rising and merging right with the sky above was to know the spell and power of this land. But the beauty of the river and of the hills, and the legend of the shepherd-god, eluded my father on that day. He fought with the bus driver over money. He gave a savage beating to two or three children. He was blatantly aggressive, more than was usual even for him, in his advances toward a married woman, a parent of one of the children who had come along on the excursion. Great deeds, great battles had occurred on the banks of that river, it was decreed by the owner and principal of the National School.

Things were stretched to the breaking point. Then one day, sometime in early '52, a life raft was thrown to him by a man from Saudi Arabia. Saudis—men in long white *thoubs*, women with

veils—were beginning to find their way to Lebanon. They were coming here for the cooler summers, for the quaint towns in the mountains, for the pleasures of the red-light district, the *Zaituna*, in Beirut. As it was told in the tale that became part of our memory, my father was in downtown Beirut, in one of the crowded cafés. This was unusual: sitting for long chats, for games of cards, for cups of thick coffee was not for him. The tranquil stereotype of a man of the Levant puffing on a water pipe in a café made hazy by smoke would have to locate another man. My father was much too restless for that. That day, he sat worried and dejected. A man from Saudi Arabia engaged him in a conversation.

Something clicked between the two men. The Saudi offered my father passage to Saudi Arabia, a visa, help with work. Oil had been discovered by American prospectors in the late 1930s. By the early 1950s, there were opportunities in Saudi Arabia for the ambitious. There was then a building boom. The Saudi was in construction. My father knew nothing about construction. But he had going for him his self-confidence and his despair. With his house and his school mortgaged, it was the prudent thing to set off for the Arabian peninsula.

For more than half a century, despair had been taking the Lebanese to West Africa, to South America, to the New World, to the automotive factories of Detroit, Michigan. There were photos of men and women who made the passage to the factories. The photos were of standard American suburban homes with American cars parked in front of them. The romance of the automobile industry had been no small one—the appeal of hourly wages and steady work, the very glamor of what the assembly lines produced. Now the Arabian Peninsula had opened up. Like *jinns*, genies, it was said, those Americans can find oil in the desert that other men had loathed, the very same desert that the

desert-dwellers were always desperate to escape. My father joined the stream of men leaving Lebanon. He decided to take the leap.

My father went to Arnoun to plead his case that a piece of land in the village should be mortgaged to help him get started in Saudi Arabia. There was a great outburst between father and son. Pieces of land were things both tangible and mystical. They were there for "black days": for illness, for old age, for times when the unknown struck. Pieces of land were the measure of men. They were sure things, while ventures to distant places were steps into the void. My grandfather's objections were overridden. My grandmother had brought land into the marriage, and my father had always been her special son, her favorite. Her son needed help, and he would get it. A roving gypsy fortune-teller had come to Arnoun a few days before my father had shown up asking for help. Gypsy fortune-tellers were thrown up by the road of Arnoun: suddenly they turned up. Everyone swore that the gypsy shysters would be expelled as soon as they made their appearance in the village. But they were always welcomed by the anxious wanting their future told, wanting to know the schemes of enemies and siblings. That heavily tattooed fortune-teller had been a slippery one: two or three hens had disappeared when she left Arnoun. But the fortune-teller had prophesied an "open road" before one of Rawshna Alawiyya's sons. Yes, the gypsy could see the son restless and in great distress. Some few ill-wishers were praying for his misfortune. But the "open road" was sure to deliver him. Where the "open road" led, the gypsy could not say. But she saw strangers bowing before him, doors leading to bliss and fulfillment flung wide open for him. The road taken, Rawshna's beloved son was sure to return to her crowned with success.

An owl was heard the night my father left the house of his parents in Arnoun. Owls were purveyors of doom. My grandmother

murmured some prayers and worried about what was to come. More alarming still, my father stepped out of the house only to return for something he had forgotten. "Ali should have sent someone to pick up his keys," my grandmother said. "The traveler should never step back over the threshold once he has embarked on a journey." A broken journey was trouble. My grandmother was full of foreboding over the entire matter—the journey to the Hijaz, the mortgaged land. But she pushed her foreboding aside. *Iblis*, Satan, played with men and women and left them prey to all kinds of fears and premonitions. But what was written would unfold, my grandmother believed. And her son's road would be open before him.

My father got what he wanted in Arnoun. He was getting a break, and so was my mother. On a rainy day, my brother and I took our meager possessions and joined her in the room with the tin roof. My father was making his final preparations for his passage to Saudi Arabia. He sent me to see if my mother was there. "You will get what you wish," he said. "You will trade a palace for a hut." (The cold, mortgaged house by the swamp did have its pretensions!) My mother wasn't home. But afraid he would change his mind and call off the whole thing, I returned to say that all was well and that she was waiting for us.

There was a place under the doorstep where my mother always left the key. We let ourselves in. When she came home at dusk *Amir Al Muminin*, Commander of the Faithful, Imam Ali, was thanked. The divorced woman had no one but *Amir al Muminin* to thank. She said that her prayers were answered: but she had more appeals to file with *Amir al Muminin*, with his sacred family of martyrs, and with the Almighty. She had lived to see Ali Ajami banished to foreign lands. Now she just wanted to

be there when news came that Ali Ibn Rawshna had been lost in God's country, that no son of Adam knew what became of him.

The Almighty gave rope, overlooked things, postponed the moment of reckoning and the moment of judgment. But my mother insisted that He was there and that He would intervene: after all, it was said in God's book that whoever has done an "atom's worth of good" shall see it and be rewarded by it, and whoever has done an atom's worth of evil shall see it as well.

Throughout a life of sorrow and toil, my mother held on to what should have been an odd proposition for her to believe in: at the root of things, there was eventual justice—reward for good deeds, retribution for cruelties. When a break came—such as this one—the hand of God was seen guiding the world. When it didn't, when there were so many dry seasons, faith persisted. No one should second-guess the order of things, she believed. For in the Quran, and in the folklore of men and women taking what was thrown at them, there was a dictum: "It may be that you hate a thing while it is good for you, and it may well be that you love a thing while it is bad for you: and God knows, whereas you do not."

My father left for Saudi Arabia unlamented by his students at the National School or by my brother and me. He had tormented my brother. Though I had slipped through the cracks, I was happy to see him go, to be rid of him.

Heavy rain fell the night my brother and I came to stay with our mother. I listened to the rain against the tin roof and was sure that it would give way. My mother slept between my brother and me. I did not know where "God's country" was, but I slept to the sound of the rain and to the thought of my father getting lost in some faraway place, of school without him, and of life without the sound of Abu Khasba's wooden leg.

—ᴍ—

The mantle of the National School passed to my youngest uncle, Abbas, who was then in his early twenties, a good decade younger than my father. He had completed his secondary school education and had lived in Beirut for a few years. He was well-liked, soft-spoken, good at sports, a beneficiary of the ease that city life had already given our clan. He was a flirt in his own shy and reticent manner: friends of his sisters were coy around him. Everything about Abbas set him apart from my father: the infectious smile for the scowl; the languid grace for the hectic fury, the dark black hair and brown skin—my grandfather's coloring and mine—for the red hair and the red face, their mother's inheritance. The one or two women who made the transition from the older to the younger brother swore by the younger brother's name.

Abbas had glimpsed a less cruel world than the one his older brothers had known. He was a step further away from the land and its merciless ways—which may account for the love he had for the village, for the pleasure he took in the hunting trips into the wilderness that surrounded Arnoun, for the thatched hut on stilts he built for himself on my grandfather's vineyard on the outskirts of Arnoun.

Abbas was younger than three of my aunts. He was loved and nurtured by them. And we were his nephews. He cared for my brother and me in his quiet, gentle way. We did not remind Abbas of a wretched marriage. When he turned up at school on a Sunday with a scout uniform—in long pants, of course—and announced that he wanted a team of Boy Scouts for the National School, it was clear that a new world had blown our way.

My uncle Abbas commuted to our school from my grandfather's home in West Beirut—this is how it was identified even

though my grandfather lived in Arnoun. It was a large house where four of my unmarried aunts lived with their two brothers.

My "grandfather's house" was a cable car—and two fares—away in a residential and quiet part of Beirut. I savored my visits there. The cable car made its way from the alleyways where I lived through the center of the city, the *Place des Martyrs*, with the neon lights, the movie houses, the brothel just barely concealed behind the shops. Then the cable car climbed beyond the city center and *Souk el Nouriyeh*, its crowded outdoor market, to West Beirut, with its cobblestone streets and large sprawling houses. To the right of the cable car climb there was the Basta quarter, the regional center of Muslim West Beirut, home of its *qabadayat*, its street toughs, and its coffee houses and mosques—the repositories of its politics. From there was *Ain al Mreisseh*, a pretty quarter adjacent to the American University of Beirut overlooking the bay and the seafront. But self-enclosed Basta, with its honeycombed streets, bore the truth of orthodox Islam and carried its banner. The *shabab*, the young men, of Basta were the zealous defenders of things Arab and things Muslim in Beirut. Basta watched the city around it—the seafront with its American University and its snack bars and its busy hotels, the Christian quarter of Achrafiyeh just on the other side of the city, the Armenian quarter farther down the hill, the southern approaches, the sand dunes of the city's outskirts with their mixed Maronite and Shia neighborhoods and their Palestinian refugee camps—with care and suspicion. Beyond Basta, just beyond the sand dunes, at the end of the cable car ride, there was a pine forest. My grandfather's house was by the pine forest.

Fouad's grandfather and his favorite uncle,
Abbas, on the streets of Beirut

The large house gave away my family's history and confusions. The vegetation in the garden was wild and unkept. The pieces of furniture didn't fit. There were old pieces—chairs, bedroom dressers, hard awkward pillows—that gave away our recent passage from the village. Other pieces—the dining room table and chairs, the embroidered tablecloth, the living room set—were of more recent vintage. The new pieces were statements of intention, messages about what my father's family was trying to be.

My aunts complained that their Beiruti neighbors were an inhospitable lot, that the neighbors would not offer a drink of water to a thirsty soul. They were sure that the Sunni Muslims

of West Beirut were miserly, that they lived in the place but were not really of it. The resourceful young women in our family set about mastering the ways of the city. They adopted the softer tones of its language, suppressed the dialect and the intonation and the words of the countryside. A gifted younger aunt of mine became a teacher in one of the city's better schools. In her own way, the young school teacher understood that she was the first of her clan to make a living in a world of "strangers" and with this came some confidence in the way she stood her ground on things that mattered to her. Into the timid household she brought some of the daring and the freedom of the city. She became an avid reader of novels. She was the first to wear high heels, to have her dresses cut by a city tailor—Luwis, the most distinguished tailor in Beirut. She insisted that this came with her job.

For her passage and for her daring, she had the warrant and protection of her father. The land had given Shaykh Muhammad the life he had wanted. He had done well by it—he had had his horses and his wanderings and his friends—but he knew that this would no longer do for his progeny. He took pride in the young woman's schooling and her aptitude for learning; he was overjoyed to hear her school principal describe her as the "flower of her school." He was not cowed or embarrassed when a brother-in-law of his taunted him and said that the shaykh had the kind of pride in his daughter that was worthy of a son. He made a pact of sorts with her: she would not be forced into a premature marriage against her will. Her older brother, Ahmad, a civil servant in the Ministry of Agriculture, himself unmarried—a subject of many winks and taunts and queries—was keen to marry off the whole group of sisters, who had come to the city and whose protector and guardian he believed he was. He hoped to marry them off early to monied Lebanese traders who worked in Africa and who

returned home in search of brides. Otherwise careful with money—a miserly man perhaps—Ahmad was known for giving costly and extravagant dinners. This was one way of putting his sisters on display, of bringing them under the scrutiny of young, eligible bachelors. The brother and his candidates were humored, but there would be no forced marriage for this young woman. Two of her five sisters, the two older ones, had given up on schooling to get married. The oldest had gone with her husband to West Africa before the move to Beirut. The second had married a sayyid who was a sergeant in the gendarmes. The two older sisters had accepted the verdict of their family: early marriage, a life lived within the limits. This middle child was different.

She turned down one suitor after another, always with an excuse at the ready: this one was too short, that one was too old, the other one came from a family of womanizers whose men had always been cruel to their wives. Ahmad threatened retribution, threatened to drag her by the hair when the time came for her to stand in the presence of a shaykh with her intended husband. But she was not easily bullied. Ahmad was a burdened man with an unpleasant disposition, but she knew he was harmless. There was a whole world outside the doorsteps of her home. So long as she held her head high, so long as she played by the rules, and her good name and reputation remained unsullied, she could go her own way. To her came the daring and novel idea that she would marry a man of her own choice, that she would marry for love.

The land was still close—way too close for young women finding their way into the world of their new city friends, discarding the attire of the land for the new styles of Beirut, reading experimental Egyptian novels, putting long hours into learning French, trying to slip through the gates of the great town without alarms and sirens giving them away as intruders on the city.

My Aunt Wajih remembered the searing mark of her passage: she had passed herself off at school as a Sunni. At age fourteen she had to submit her national identity card to her school. Her identity card, like all identity cards in our country, had specified her religion and her sect. The young schoolgirl, anxious to cover her tracks, had panicked: she smeared her identity card with a blot of ink, covered the dreaded Shia label that gave her away. She got caught at it. The school principal, who was fond of her, would forget the episode, forget that she was tampering with government documents. It was never easy slipping through the gates.

The past was never far enough. We had not yet found the way out of the clan and the webs of the clan. The peace of this settled city was not ours. The chatter and the smoke of its neighborhood coffee houses; the backgammon players testing their skills on the sidewalks; the merchants and the clerks returning from their shops and offices in the center of the city, newspaper under one arm, watermelon under the other; the quiet evenings and family gatherings on the balconies: the ways of the *commerçants* were not ours. We had older relatives—women with tattoos on their hands and their chins, women with head covers, men with red fezzes carrying baskets of figs and buckets of yogurt—who showed up right when the new city was about to be mastered, arriving unannounced to remind us, to remind my brave aunts juggling two different worlds, where we had come from. Abu Fawzi, the old great-uncle with the red fez and the red face, came to West Beirut with a live chicken as a present for his embarrassed nieces.

My Aunt Sakiba—herself destined to be a spinster, guiding her countless nephews and nieces on their uncertain passage to modernity—kept track of the great urban families that ordered the small world of West Beirut and disposed of its public affairs. Years had gone into the making of this tranquility, this

routine. Years had confirmed the hegemony of the seven families of Beirut, of all those names that she ticked off—the Beyhums, Douks, Tayyars, Ardatis, Nusulis, Fakhuris, Najas.

My Great-uncle Youssef, though, made his own peace with the city. Free of the bravado and the snickers with which so many of his relatives had approached the alien city, Youssef became a dandy. He was a loan shark who made a good living off the usurious rates he charged; he had land and some money. In his time and place, Youssef was a man who made heads turn. He had a mistress in West Beirut, Hayat, a handsome, married, middle-aged woman. Most likely Youssef was the father of Hayat's three daughters. Hayat's husband hovered somewhere in the background, but he always dropped out of sight when Youssef was around, when, as was their habit, Youssef and Hayat sat on her balcony at dusk for coffee and conversation. This is how I recall them so many years later: Youssef in his pajamas, sipping his Turkish coffee on Hayat's balcony, she by his side. I had seen no more tranquil relationship in the family world around me: the peace of Hayat's world, its settled grace, had been transmitted to the man from the countryside. He had taken that peace and made it his own. I could not have understood how daring the middle-aged Beiruti woman was. Hayat had no patience with the hypocrisies and the pretenses of the place: she looked past them, disdained the gossip-mongers, savored Youssef's presence in her life. And the loan shark—quick to close in on his victims, merciless toward those who had put up beloved pieces of land for collateral but were unable to meet their obligations—showered the polished and self-assured woman with his attention and his favors.

My Great-Uncle Youssef was fond of thick, black Turkish coffee. Hayat sat on the balcony reading Youssef's future in the

intricate markings that the sediment left at the bottom of the cup. Here she followed the line that led to a happy outcome. There she saw a bird bearing him a piece of news from afar. It must be a letter from his son. Ahmad, who had quit the country to make his fortune in Venezuela, Youssef thought. Somewhere the sediment congealed into what Hayat took to be the frowning face of his half-brother who envied him his land and good fortune and peace of mind and was threatening to take him to court once again over a contested piece of land.

Nowhere in the sediment was Hayat able to see Youssef's premature death. Death came to him unannounced, with no early warnings; it may have been heart trouble. Hayat, a woman of Beirut, laid Youssef to rest in our village. The woman of the city—a woman of beauty and poise—was overcome with grief. There was no need to hire professional wailers for that funeral. The quiet, striking woman disheveled her hair, tore at her clothes, spoke to the dead man, gently rebuking him for leaving her brokenhearted and alone so early in life. The Arnounis had prided themselves on their ability to give the dead a decent burial. Hayat, the woman of the city, put Youssef's people to shame on the day he was buried right next to his parent's mausoleum, by the pond with the cracked surface.

III

My mother trusted the Almighty with making the world right and with settling the score with my father. Her God was a great avenger. But there were things to be done, and she did them with zest and determination.

She had deep wells of patience and fortitude, and she had her Singer sewing machine, her prized possession—and her weapon. The Singer had been given to her first husband as part of her dowry. It had been meant for a prosperous home, bought from an agent who roamed the towns and villages in the country and who knew the people of means who could afford a purchase of that kind. My mother had taken to her sewing machine and become a skilled seamstress. Now after the two divorces, and the abrupt passage to the city, it had come in handy. She earned a living by repairing and patching up heaps of secondhand US Army-Navy surplus clothes for a nearby wholesaler.

Her work was not a dark secret. Secrets could not be kept in packed alleyways. It was only that my mother was careful about

her pride and ours. She was not about to go out and do factory work as other women in our neighborhood did. The work was difficult and demanding, piecemeal. But she never complained. She enjoyed the quick calculations I came up with to keep track of her daily earnings (the arithmetic learned at school being put to good use). At times she asked for help in threading a needle. These requests were her small bids for attention. She asked for help by saying that her eyes were surely failing her, that her best years were behind her. But the complaint was said with a twinkle in her eyes and perhaps a touch of vanity about her endurance and her vitality.

After her daily quota at the sewing machine was done, she was ready to step outdoors, to give the hawker a piece of her mind over the quality of his produce or to haggle over the price he asked for his vegetables. My mother was a great believer in the skewers of grilled meat. It was the food of privilege, of wealth. In Arnoun, she had begrudged my grandfather his excursions to the butcher of Nabatiyya and the abandon with which he feasted on grilled skewers of meat. Now she made her own trips to the butcher. My brother had become fond of Pepsi-Cola. She was ready to concede him his bargain: enough skewers of lamb for one bottle of Pepsi-Cola—Depsi-Cola, as she called it. When oranges were in season she took one of her brisk walks to the orchard at the outskirts of the neighborhood. And there, she either bought regular oranges, or she turned to the cheaper, defective oranges. She loved to make sandwiches of bread and oranges; she took pride in the combination, treasured it as her own creation.

My mother could not deliver the world. She could not solve the riddles of arithmetic that we had to do. She knew nothing of the foreign language we were trying to master, the language of the *Ingliz*. Food was what she knew and what she could deliver. We

were going beyond her—that she knew and accepted and wanted. But she wanted to give what she could and what was within her reach. I knew what importance she attached to food.

My earliest rebellions were outbursts against her "peasant food." These were dishes and items of the land now behind us: lentil mixed with bulghur wheat and what struck me as huge amounts of onion; bulghur with tomatoes; jam made of the figs of the South; *dibs*, pomegranate molasses. These were what my mother had grown up with and what she knew. On rare occasions, she prepared these dishes. When she did, she had an open rebellion on her hands. We would not eat the peasant food, the villager's food, my brother and I.

"*Bukra*, tomorrow will be a better day," my mother often said. Any exchange between my mother and I, her youngest, turned into something to go to sleep on:

"When can I have a bicycle of my own?"

"When my ship comes in."

"When will your ship come in?"

"*Bukra*, tomorrow."

"And when can I have blue long pants?"

"*Bukra*, with the bicycle."

"Can I see as many films as I want?"

"*Bukra*, you can do that."

Now and then after Abu Hamza, the neighbor from the town of Baalbek, had won the lottery, my mother was talked into buying lottery tickets. I spent her imaginary winnings many a time. There were promises of endless supplies of blue long pants, of a bright red bicycle, of the biggest soccer ball anywhere in sight, and of the most spectacularly colored kite any boy had ever flown.

The Singer sewing machine hummed along. Everywhere there were piles of US Army olive drab fatigues, navy blue shirts,

uniforms with stripes, uniforms of corporals and sergeants, uniforms without stripes. Not so long after my father left for Saudi Arabia, my mother's labor was beginning to pay off. We left the room with the tin roof and moved into a larger room in a two-story house on a more crowded street. "It is closer to everything, and the winter rains will not be so hard on us," my mother said.

We lived on the first floor. There was another room on the same floor. It was inhabited by Abu Abdu, a delightful retired Syrian soldier, his wife, two daughters, and two sons. We shared with the family a toilet and a kitchen. As it turned out, Umm Abdu, the woman in the household, was from my mother's town and belonged to the same large clan. Abu Abdu's Syrian homeland was behind him, as were stories of old adventures—adventures in distant places, in times past. No two versions of the same story were alike. I conspired with one of his willing children to trip him up. When we changed the outcome or the locale of a story, he joined in and improvised on the old versions. The tales came to an end when Umm Abdu told the "wretched Damascene" to wrap it up and do something useful around the house.

The two daughters—statuesque and beautiful young women who wore skirts and blouses of whatever color and cut they preferred—were in their early teens. There was an exciting hint of scandal to their behavior. They were free with their headscarves: they wore them and discarded them at will. There were young men trailing them in the morning to the factories where they worked and showing up in the alleyway when the girls returned in the evening.

The two boys in the family were a bit older than my brother and me. One of them was a roving photographer who roamed the streets and beaches of Beirut, snapped photos of unsuspecting pedestrians, insisted with his own blend of pleading and

intimidation that they had asked for the photo, and then hounded them until they acquiesced and paid up for the photo they never asked for. The second child was a harmless "tough" who peddled lottery tickets but could never stick to it. The beach, his sole passion, beckoned him. He was an accomplished swimmer and formidable on a paddle board. His mother took great pride in his height, and she was willing to forgive him when he failed to come through with his little share of money for the household. Saadallah had a simple view of schooling. Schools were for wimps, he declared. He was ready to help me cut school at any time to take me along to the beach.

In the midst of all this, my mother insisted on her distinction and ours. I grew up with tales—tales of the valor of the Abdullah men, of the fiber of the women, of generous homes open to guests from places near and far, of hundreds of riders arriving at Khiam for the weddings and funerals of her childhood. She spoke of the wealth, the *khirat*, of Khiam, of its fruits and vegetables. No one was miserly in Khiam. No one "hugged the piaster for dear life" in my mother's town and my mother's valley. They loved life, the Khiamis. It was the best of times, my mother's time in Khiam. There was a Khiami accent, a Khiami manner of speech. No sooner had my mother plunged into the tales of Khiam, something special within her came to life. Never a pretentious or self-conscious woman, her Khiami accent became more pronounced and her laughter heartier.

There was a tale my mother loved: it was her favorite and mine. It was a tale of her young brother, Bahij. Bahij was in prison. He was a folk hero among the Abdullahs. A few years back, about the time of my birth, Bahij had made a stand for the Abdullahs against *ahl al balad*, the commoners of the town. There were eternal feuds between *ahl al balad* and the Abdullahs.

We didn't know much about *ahl al balad* and what they wanted. The tale never bothered with such things. I assumed what the Abdullahs had assumed: that *ahl al balad* were the rabble, the enemies. The tale said that *ahl al balad* were getting "cheeky" and difficult to deal with, that they were challenging the turf and the prerogatives of the Abdullahs, that they no longer knew their limits and their "place." (The world had begun to batter Khiam's walls: trouble had come to paradise.)

A sinister figure by the name of Ta'an al Basha led *ahl al balad* in their challenge to the authority of the Abdullahs. Ta'an had joined the gendarmes, had become a sergeant. He bore the Abdullahs, the principal landed family in his town, the resentment of a "commoner" on the rise. Ta'an had made common cause with another political family in the district of which Khiam was a part. Ta'an and my Uncle Bahij had traded harsh words. The words were their testimonies; the duel had to be joined the right way. A man had to have his say on such occasions. The eloquence of men was no small matter. Ta'an, the insolent commoner, delivered the word of the challenger: men had put up with the Abdullahs and now they would no more. He, Ta'an, was the executioner, and he would make the Abdullahs know the bitter taste of defeat. Bahij reminded Ta'an of his wretched origins, of times when Ta'an's parents turned up at the doorsteps of the Abdullahs for a bit of wheat or for a small favor. The honor of the women was no doubt taken up by the two men as they performed the dance of death. The honor of the women always came up when men drew lines. This is how men went at one another. Bahij said that no bride from *ahl al balad* had ever walked a "girl" into her husband's home. All had lain down with the Abdullah men. Even the dead were exhumed on this occasion, summoned back to life, their deeds and warts recalled.

The two men had pushed it to the limit. There was no return. Some fights left men a way out, a small exit, some room for maneuver, a crack that men of goodwill could work with to separate the would-be combatants. Some fights didn't. This one didn't. When the dust of the battle cleared, Ta'an and several of his men were left dead in the center of Khiam.

The honor of the Abdullahs had been salvaged. Bahij had bought time for his clan—time for the evening chatter to go on, for the languid tales to be told, for the hollow pride to be felt. He had given yarn to those deadly and endearing Abdullah delusions. A world was on its way, had indeed arrived. It was a world of money and commerce, of government examinations, of men running away from Lebanon to distant places, giving it their furious best and returning with a handful of money to sink in land, in new buildings, in schools where their children were scrubbed clean of the village ways. But the Abdullahs had remained faithful to a dying world. They knew who they were, where their dead were buried. They had their gaze fixed on the past: they had a narrative of themselves that ennobled them.

The Abdullah tales of my uncle Bahij's exploits edited out the details of his years in prison—of the privation, of the cruelty. Those tales of Bahij, spun at dusk, had never bothered with the kind of life he had led. Rioters had once taken over the Ramle Prison in West Beirut, killed some of their guards. That kind of knowledge—reports of overcrowding in the prison, complaints about the food, about the cruelty of the guard—had come my way through the newspapers. But in the Abdullah stories, Bahij was glamored: that was the way of my mother's people.

The Abdullahs were making their way to Beirut. We would see much of them in the years to come. It was instant familiarity. The clan had no place in its world for privacy: one belonged to

a large network. The man or woman who just kissed you on the cheek, whom you had just laid eyes on for the first time, picked up an old thread, resumed an old, long-established intimacy. The Abdullahs came with their languid tales and their incredible self-confidence. Their men were the bravest of men. Their women, they said, were "sisters of men." Sisters of men were the toughest of women. They were the best at ululation, at making those piercing noises of joy intended for the ears of the ill-wishers. They were the most expressive at funerals: good at disheveling their hair, tearing at their dresses, wailing for the "beloved" uncle who was loathed when he was alive. Sisters of men kept homes intact when their mighty husbands landed in prison or took off for distant places.

My uncle Bahij's children were growing up without him. He had walked into prison a young man only to walk out of it ten years later with his youth behind him. But what of it? The Abdullahs said that prisons were for men. And, besides, there were tales of Bahij now and then let out of his prison by his guards for a visit to his family or for an outing on the town or for an occasional visit to the brothel in downtown Beirut. The Abdullahs had their consolations.

The duel between my Uncle Bahij and Ta'an had followed us here. Ta'an's sister had turned up in our neighborhood in an alleyway behind ours. For a while, my mother was agitated over the matter. She wanted us to be on guard and keep away from Ta'an's sister's children. "We had a blood-feud as deep as the river," she said. "And blood never sleeps." It was the Abdullah imagery and the Abdullah drama. It was Khiam's passion wishing to give itself another lease on life. But here, so far away in these alleyways, nothing happened between us and Ta'an's sister's children: we hit the same streets, hung out at the same movie theaters (the

only two in the neighborhood), tried to work our way into the same soccer matches. We were no doubt wrestling with the same Arabic grammar.

The Abdullah tales told, the glasses of tea filled and refilled, the card games played, the cot rolled on the floor for the visiting relatives. My mother's tales belonged to some cozy past where men and women were whole. They were of a world that knew only of itself, that acknowledged only itself. But the cobwebs were being blown away by powerful winds. Everywhere around us, people without memories of some fabled past were remaking their world, hacking away at the old world. My mother and the people of her valley were clinging to their pride and memory.

I loved the Abdullahs, but their stories were not mine and could not be made mine. I had gone to my mother's town: I had waded through its streams; I had joined my Abdullah cousins on the waterwheel in a magnificent spring nearby; I had climbed the almond tree in the backyard of my grandparent's home. (The spring and the almond trees had always been themes in my mother's tales. They were already familiar to me when I encountered them for the first time. I "recognized" them.) But the Abdullah stories could not sustain me. I had grown up amidst the Ajamis, a more sullen and driven lot. For the Abdullah talk of the past, there was the Ajami talk of visas and passage to distant places, of examinations, of land mortgaged and money made, of the opportunities that beckoned in Liberia and Sierra Leone or in the hellish heat of Saudi Arabia. My grandfather indulged a tale as far as his stern temperament would permit. Then, invariably, he cut teller and tale off with one of his favorite peasant sayings: "At examination time, a man will be honored or dishonored." There was another saying of the land which he liked: "He who sowed

will reap; he who searched will find." We had been given ideas and ambitions—and a great fear that failure was never far behind.

While the Abdullah's told meandering tales, my father's family spoke in clipped tones. We were a people of a harsh, rocky ridge. We had the rhythm of the tobacco crop on which the family depended and on which it always dwelled. The garlands of tobacco dangling from the ceiling in my grandfather's home—waiting for the inspectors of the Régie to come and assign them a price before hauling them off to the factories and warehouses in Beirut—inspired no love, no affection between man, the land, and what man grew on the land. My father's family grew tobacco they never smoked.

The tales troubled me for yet another reason. I could not allow myself to make them my own without slipping fully into my mother's universe. A struggle always raged between a father and a mother over the forming of a son's sensibility, over "making a man" out of him. So long as both parents were there under one roof, the struggle could be concealed, and the son could alternate between the maternal hearth and the stern domain of his father. There was a moment in every boy's life when he was banished by his father out of the world of women, when he could no longer walk in on their conversations, when he could no longer just wander in as the women—mother, aunts, their friends—were removing the hair on their legs with a homemade concoction of lemon and sugar to help himself to samples of the delicious stuff before the women put it to better use. Hitherto, a boy walked in as secrets were spilled; as the future was read and foretold by deciphering the sediment left in the small cups of thick coffee; as the ways and follies of men were dissected by women who alternated between describing them as cruel and dangerous hyenas and, then, depicting the same men as malleable material that a

bright, clever woman with guile and some looks could mold and play with while pretending that the fierce man was the source of all authority.

No attention was paid, no routine interrupted, when "the boy" wandered into the circle of women. Majida, the beauty in the extended family, would leave her skirt above her knees and the boy could, with some affected innocence, take in the view. The "almond-eyed" widow, Afifa, scantily dressed in her black embroidered slip that showed under her dress, went on streaking her hair with henna, tossing it backward as she insisted that the man rumored to have slipped into her house several times this last month was really a braggart, who had tasted the pleasure of her company in his dreams. This boyhood bliss could not last. Maybe it was the change in the boy's voice or the faint outline of a moustache that gave him away. Or perhaps it was the clumsiness with which he feigned his disinterest when Majida caught him following the outline of her body against her tight dress. A sharp-tongued woman may have been the one who decided the matter on the day that she wondered whether the boy really belonged in the sanctum of women.

Then the banishment came. It had to come. Only eunuchs and castrated men stayed in the domain of women. Our own folk history passed on by scribes and storytellers was uncompromising on this point: ruin came to males who stayed too long among women. After all, Shaharzad had entangled the King Shahryar with her thousand and one tales. Each night Shaharzad told the tale and then "perceived the dawn of day and ceased to say her permitted say." Next evening, she was ready with the same yarn: "It has reached me, O auspicious king, that the King of China…."

Boys had to be dragged against their will into the company of men. A boy had to step out of the insinuating talk of women

into the bluster of men. No demands had been made on the boy in the gathering of women. His was an illicit presence. He could slip in and out of the tales; he could enjoy the talk even as he derided it. Once forced into the gatherings of men, the boy was not a participant either. He had to undergo a long period of apprenticeship, as the mighty men described how they "kicked open the doors" of the ministries and government agencies. He had to be there, fully there, as the visiting obscurantist man of religion pronounced that the Quran had anticipated the telephone and the airplane. He had to bite his tongue as Abu Fawzi, emphatic Great-Uncle Abu Fawzi, with the red fez and the red face, told the boy that he was still hopelessly "green" and that he had many years to go before he could have an opinion on the issues of the day. The boy may have read an article in the daily paper on the subject on which Abu Fawzi was so emphatic. But the world of Abu Fawzi and of men like him came complete and could not be challenged.

There was nothing the boy could do or say as the conversation among the men continued: "Yes, your eminence the cleric, Allah is All knowing, and we his humble creatures know so little; you are right that the world was born complete and the Quran anticipated the tape-recorder. The Holy Book did say that men, on the day of Resurrection, will hear their voices and their words uttered while on their earthly sojourn. As for you, sir, the man who kicked open the door of the Ministry of Education, rest assured there was no one around while you shuffled in with endless government forms and petitions and pleaded with His excellency the Bureaucrat to look into your case. And you, Abu Fawzi, yes don't worry, the boy does know the saying—the boy knows so many sayings, he knows so little else—'older than you by a day, wiser than you by a year.'" Once banished from the world of women, the boy had more of this to look forward to.

But I had no father around to banish me from my mother's bosom. I was in my mother's world. Even the physical space I needed to maintain a separation was not there. I must have been a child of six when I first confronted, with terror and bewilderment, my mother's menstrual cycle. We were a people who maintained silence over such matters. I was assured that she was well, that such things befell women, that she was in no great danger. It was a monthly "habit," I was told. Having seen what I had seen, I was left to wonder and to worry.

I had to keep my own distance from my mother's world and my mother's talk. I could not put on male airs, hide behind a father's world while partaking of the warmth, of the seduction, of the women's world. I had to perform my own banishment. I had to do it without shrillness, without overdoing it, without dismissing the Abdullah women and their Abdullah talk, without warring with my mother. I was not sure I could be rescued, whether I could find a way out once I had given myself over to my mother's world. There was a boy-king in a neighboring realm, Hussein of Jordan: when his enemies wanted to belittle him, they dismissed him as Hussein Ibn Zein, Hussein the son of Zein. Zein was his mother.

The Abdullah talks of previous splendor were one side of my mother's coping with her world. Another was her faith in her two sons, her stubborn assertion that we were unlike the others around us, that we would be going places. My mother insisted on this. She did so with a passion that belied her worries. Our neighbor, Umm Abdu, had said that no one was better than anyone else in this neighborhood. It was not clear to her eyes why my mother should put on airs and speak of better things to come for her children.

The boy's father, Umm Abdu said, was busy with his new wife and his new children. Umm Abdu saw things that were easy to see. There was no evidence of money coming our way from Saudi Arabia. Sooner or later, when the free elementary education provided us at the National School came to an end, we too, said our neighbor, would have to do something practical with our lives to make ends meet.

But my mother was made of different material. Her imagination was bigger than her reach. She had an idol and example for us. A young man from the Abdullah family, with plenty of land and wealth to his father's name, had gone off to Paris and returned with an engineering degree. When I was seven, Hussein Effendi Abdullah, engineer Hussein Abdullah, had been elected to Parliament and was even appointed to a cabinet post. Hussein Abdullah was larger, more polished, than the town he came from. He had become a legend in his own time, had crossed the line behind which his people lived and walked into the world of the city: he married a woman of Beirut. His people always came to him as supplicants in need of favors.

My mother borrowed the example of Hussein Abdullah, held it before us. Miracles do happen, she believed. The cruelty of the father could be gotten around, lived with, tolerated. Besides, my father was away. When he returned, he would still be faced with the claims of two sons. My father's eldest born to my stepmother was a girl. And surely Ali Ajami was not foolish enough to place his bets on a daughter. No one, not even Ali Ajami, my mother said, wanted to be known by the deeds of a daughter. If a man's luck held, a daughter married well, kept a low profile, and kept out of sight. The world, said my divorced mother, belonged to men.

My father's second child born to my step-mother had partial paralysis in his legs and arms. That, too, sealed the matter for my

mother. Her two sons, my brother and I, would remain claimants to whatever was there to be claimed in my father's hands.

Appearances had to be kept and were of great importance. I fancied some of the shirts that my mother repaired. I liked the stripes. But I was not to wear old shirts. I was a "schoolboy," and I was to wear new clothes, my mother insisted. My mother was stubborn about such matters. Old clothes were for others. They were for our neighbors. And besides, old clothes were a bad omen. You become the clothes you wear. We were on a tightrope. She must have known that were we to fall, there was really no way of knowing where matters could end. My brother and I were to be reminded at every turn of "who we were." Our clothes were a message to my grandfather, to my father's family, to anyone who cared, that we were aspirants for something better.

We were soon joined by my mother's three children from her first marriage. The land coughed them up one by one. First came my half-brother, Ali, the middle child of the three. He was followed by my half-sister, Rasmiyya, my mother's oldest; then came my half-sister Raqiyya. We rolled three more mattresses out on the floor.

The three of them said very little about their life in their father's village. Their father had married again. (He would marry six or seven women in his lifetime.) It was clear that they had suffered. You could see it in their eyes. They internalized it, acquiesced in it, displayed it as though to ward off further suffering. Theirs had been a cruel father.

They were simple country people. Just as the smells of the land clung to the scarf of Rasmiyya, the ways of the land, the politeness, clung to my brother Ali. They spoke the dialect and the words of the land that was to our backs and theirs—the dialect I loathed, the dialect I associated with our peasant ways.

Ali was fourteen years old when he joined us. He was a quiet, shy boy. Our country asked of men to be roosters and braggarts. A rooster this one wasn't. It was easy to see that he must have been hounded by his father. He breathed the fresh air of the city with an appreciation that told of previous oppression. He took up wrestling (the more graceful Greco-Roman style), and became a local celebrity in our neighborhood. There was no explanation for the wrestling talent. He joined an athletic club, and the wrestling talent just emerged. He found work in a bakery. Bakery work was difficult labor, hellish during the summer months. He had to wake up before dawn, and he was a heavy sleeper. The windup alarm clock piercing the silence before dawn was the torment of his life. But he put up with it for three or four years. He brought home his weekly pay and gave it to my mother. And every day he brought home two kilograms of bread, his last batch, fresh and wrapped in a newspaper.

Ali was less "glamorous" than working boys his age or a little older who braved their way to the whorehouse in the center of the city when they received their weekly wages. He stayed away from card games, from circles of gamblers who gathered around in our neighborhood and placed their bets on things ranging from flipping coins to pinball machines, to shaking and opening bottles of soda pop and trying to make the soda foam and go over the edges. He did none of these things that appealed to me in those days. But he was a boy in his teens who held onto a heavy quilt before a hard day's work—a boy without illusions and without a safety net.

Rasmiyya was a quiet and beautiful young woman, a bit taller than my mother, with auburn hair and friendly, clear brown eyes. Rasmiyya, my mother said, was a *shariffa*, a descendant of the Prophet. Her prayers, I was told, were answered by her "grandfather," the Prophet Muhammad. Those who loved and favored her

would find good fortune along their way; those who tormented her were likely to suffer. It seemed that she always looked past the ways of the city, communed with an older and more settled world than that of the hectic alleyways.

Rasmiyya found steady work in a chocolate factory. She was a hard and honest worker. Often she favored me with pieces of chocolate. On special occasions she returned from work with my favorite—a rooster made out of chocolate.

Raqiyya was in every way Rasmiyya's opposite. She was assertive, flighty, and unpredictable. There was no explanation for her wild temperament. She had issued from the womb of the same mother, grown up on the same land, in the household of the same sayyid: she, too, was a *shariffa*. But *tabia'a*, nature, my people said, had its ways and mysteries. My mother worried about Raqiyya; she worried where her wildness would lead. Mothers had an eye for this kind of potential trouble in their daughters.

My mother watched and worried about the younger of my two half-sisters. My mother's premonition of trouble would be borne out. It came in small ways, gradually. Raqiyya could not be relied upon to return from work on time; there were days when she didn't go to work at all. She was seen talking to a man in the neighborhood. Raqiyya was pulled into the orbit of our neighbor's daughters, Hayat and Dhia—young women my mother liked, but in whose "character" she didn't have much faith. A few times, Raqiyya was beaten by Ali. The beatings bought a few days of caution. But she was a stubborn soul.

My mother fought to keep Raqiyya on the safe side of the line. But the new ways of the city overwhelmed her. Raqiyya soon went over the edge. One day she went off into one of the Palestinian refugee camps on the outskirts of the city, on its southern approaches, just beyond the pine forest and the settled neighborhoods. There,

she fell for a young Palestinian. Headstrong, she wouldn't be deterred. She would marry the man of her choice, join his family. She dropped out of our world and adopted the culture—and even the dialect—of her husband's world. It took a few years before she was forgiven by my mother. She had married outside the faith, to a Sunni Muslim. She had married a Palestinian—a man with no land of his own, with no nationality.

Raqiyya broke out of the net. Ali and Rasmiyya remained in my life. They took a vicarious kind of pleasure and pride in my school supplies: the work I brought home, the bag in which I carried the colored crayons I liked, my crinkled notebook, my reading primer or history text. Rasmiyya loved to look at English script: she thought that only wizards could manage so strange an enterprise as a foreign tongue. When she discovered that her name translated into English remained the same, she was deflated, let down by the English language.

My full brother and I may have been "the future," but Ali and Rasmiyya bore the burden of the present. We stood on their shoulders. My mother's world was based on the toil of the older children and on the promise of the younger ones.

—⚊—

Tales of her and her family's past were an antidote to life in the alleyway. But my mother stayed close to my father's family: it was part of her way of protecting her sons' claims. She was there for the Ajami weddings and funerals. She was there when there were scandals to be hushed up and when there were triumphs to be celebrated. She was at hand for what life threw at men and women. She was there when amulets had to be fetched to keep the husbands at peace with their wives. And she was always in Arnoun

when there was work to be done that required her labor. She put up with my grandmother's temper and commands. She was too realistic and shrewd a woman to ask for my grandparent's affection: there wasn't much affection offered in Arnoun. All she asked for was acceptance, an alliance to see my brother and I through. "My boys are sons of a son," she said. "No one in this family can walk away from them and lay claim to a shred of honor."

This was something my grandfather understood and believed. After my father's departure to Saudi Arabia, we were to see a good deal of my grandfather. To my mother, his visits to us in the city were events of great importance. She must have taken them as proof of her place and the place of her sons in her former husband's family, proof that she—and we—belonged to my father's clan. She would spare no expense in welcoming my grandfather. His favorite dishes were prepared. My mother was glad to go into debt—to borrow from the butcher or to pay the asking price of the hawker of fruits and vegetables: there was no time to haggle over prices. She was eager to please the patriarch of Arnoun.

My mother knew that there had always been a special place for me in my grandfather's view of his descendants. It had always been said in the Ajami household that I had something of him in me, that I took after him. What little I had learned in school—bits of grammar, fragments of stilted history, the poetry we were made to memorize—I was encouraged to recite before my grandfather. "He will be there for you, he will do you honor and carry in your footsteps," my grandfather was told. "May he never be deprived of your support and affection."

I took in what was expected of me. I learned it and inhaled it at an early age. I was a step-son, son of a divorced woman. But if I tried hard enough, I could get my grandfather's acceptance

and attention: I could belong to my father's family. My father was not around, but there were always discussions of his imminent return, of the prominence he placed on schooling and success. There were, after all, his newspaper clippings and other tales of his ambitions. Love and acceptance were contingent on performance: they were given and they were withheld. An assertive boy—good at school, good at memorizing things, good at command performances—had a place in the family scheme of things, was "counted" and kept track of. I pushed my older brother aside, outtalked him; I memorized more than he did. I was the one my mother trotted out before my grandfather and the rest of my mother's family.

My mother's campaign was relentless. And in her campaign, Shaykh Muhammad was assigned a prominent place. She needed my grandfather's support if and when my father returned from Saudi Arabia. She knew that my grandfather's voice would come in handy when my brother and I had to make our way to secondary school. This my mother knew: children needed protection against capricious fathers, and she was not there to provide the shield. Women did this for their sons in her old world and in our new one. But this was a function she could no longer perform. Others had to do this. And none was more qualified than my grandfather. She wanted to make sure that the shaykh would come through for her and for her two sons. The man in Saudi Arabia would have to face his own father in future duels.

It was on one of my grandfather's visits to the city that an issue of religious custom and practice came up: my brother's circumcision and mine. No one thought of circumcising infants at birth. Most of us had been delivered by midwives, by neighbors, by relatives. The circumcision was put off into later years. But my mother had put it off for too long. Such were the follies of boys

being raised by women. Now my grandfather said that the postponement had gone far enough; he wanted the deed done before his next visit.

I must have been approaching my eighth year when it was my turn to submit to the circumciser. On that dreaded day, I took no consolation from the assurance of the words *al mutahir al Qanuni*, legal circumciser, scribbled on the side of his bag. I doubted whether his legality would offer any relief from the terror of it all.

Several boys in my neighborhood had gone through the ritual before me. After the brutal deed, they had appeared among us in white frocks; they had walked with great care and kept the frocks as far away from their bodies as they could. Now it was my brother's turn and mine. We ran toward the open fields by the railroad tracks, but a couple of older boys in the neighborhood caught up with us and brought us back in tears, pleading for mercy. To her eternal credit, my mother could not take the sight and preferred to stay outdoors and wait for the ordeal to end. The deed done, some simple ointment was applied to stop the bleeding.

My mother extended what sympathy she could. There was a little celebration, a ritual: my mother distributed sugar-coated almonds to the neighbors. For days, it was sheer hell to urinate. And there was the piercing pain every time the flowing long shirt I wore came anywhere close to my body, and the terror mixed with the blood.

We had our religious ritual. But we were not instructed in the faith. My school, and schools similar to it, taught nothing of the Shia faith or of Islam itself. My generation was not instructed in the Quran. The Quran was an affair of older men, lettered men. Religion was less about doctrine than about the customs, about the mortadella we were not supposed to eat at the Muslim

butcher. And of course, it was about the circumciser with his scissors and his black bag.

Most of what I knew of religion had come through my mother's laments and through some of the rituals I had observed in my grandparent's home in Arnoun: I knew that *tahara*, purity, and *najasa*, impurity, were important to my grandmother. I had observed her go through the ablutions before prayer. My grandmother had always been careful with water, making sure it was not wasted, that the Arnouni women who helped around the house were not frivolous with it. It was during the ablution that both my grandparents seemed to use water with abandon. Prayer had to be approached in a state of purity and cleanliness. This was the Shia fear of defilement: our people were known for it. An exasperated Presbyterian missionary, an American, who roamed my birthplace a century before I was born, who came right up to Beaufort, noted this excessive fear. The obsession, he wrote, "carried into many other things besides clean and unclean meat, drinks, apparel, and vessels for household use…You never contract friendships with persons who will neither eat, drink with, nor visit you, and into whose houses you cannot enter without contracting or imparting defilement."

This phobia was not as crippling when I was growing up. It could no longer be indulged or honored. Our cocoon had been torn up. What remained was the nervousness of a people braving old limits, giving the old fear new names and forms. I knew of religion what was to be picked up by a child who listened to the tales of the imams. The imams were invoked by my mother and appealed to every time I tripped up. From early childhood, the imams were asked to look after me. Two of the twelve were to be on my right and left. One of them was to hover above me. And I, hopeless in matters of religion, disappointed the superstitious

woman by saying that surely with so many imams in the way, I would trip and fall, unable to play soccer or go about my daily business.

I was about nine years old then when my mother set out for her first visit to the shrine of Sitt Zaynab, the daughter of Imam Ali and his wife Fatima, the Prophet's daughter. Zaynab was loved by all the defeated and the vanquished. Widows and divorced women and ailing old women identified with Zaynab, who had died brokenhearted for all the suffering that befell her family. She was there in the plain of Kerbala during that seventh century battle when her beloved brother, Imam Hussein, was murdered and trampled by the horses, when all his younger brothers and even an infant child of his were killed. It was Zaynab who offered up Hussein's body to God and told her grandfather, the Prophet Muhammad, that his grandson had been martyred. Zaynab had accompanied the caravan of sorrow and defeat, the surviving women and children, *ahl al bayt*, from Kerbala to the city of Kufa in Iraq, then to Damascus, to the court of the heartless ruler, the Caliph Yazid. Zaynab was the one who had saved the life of Imam Hussein's surviving son, the fourth imam, Zayn al Abidin, "the adornment of the Faithful." She had covered his body with hers on the plain of Kerbala after the gruesome massacre of the rest of the Prophet's family. She had died in Syria and was buried on the outskirts of Damascus.

Zaynab's was the quintessential Shia tale of virtue and defeat and lament. It was a perfect tale for my mother. She had prepared for the journey to Damascus, saved for it. In the years to come, the visits became more frequent, the periods of stay longer. My mother went to the shrine to fulfill a *nidr*, a vow. But the *nidr* was only part of it. My mother was a believer. She wanted to be present in the courtyard of the shrine, to hang onto the gilt-edged

railing of Zaynab's mausoleum. She wanted the added comfort. Believers from the far corners of the earth, she said, will be there. They will come from as far away as Iraq, from Persia, the country of the Ajam. There was no need to worry about her: she will be among other petitioners and believers. And Zaynab, the daughter of the Commander of the Faithful, will wipe her and their tears, see them through difficult times, look after their children, avenge the wrongs done to them.

Many roads, my mother said, shall be opened to me by Zaynab. She will hear and know and understand. Zaynab, no doubt, heard a great deal on that visit about Ali, the son of Rawshna. The daughter of our first imam, *Bint Amir al Muminin*, the granddaughter of the Prophet Muhammad, was told of the suffering of *bint al Abadila*, the daughter of the Abdullahs. It must have taken no time to establish intimacy between the revered seventh-century woman and the humble figure, the divorced woman, who came to her shrine. God may have been distant, awesome, intimidating, but Zaynab was a fellow sufferer. She, like my mother, had known hardship. She, too, had "lost her nest" and was condemned to exile. She had lived to see the rabble inherit earthly kingdoms, put on airs, strut at court. Fate had "heaped up all the sorrows of the world" in Zaynab's lap. My mother was sure her own history was a variation on the old tale. Zaynab was asked to help protect my mother's children from the evil eye, from the schemes of the ill-wishers. That was all the humble petitioner, she who had no other pillar of support, asked of Zaynab.

Word reached my grandmother Rawshna that my mother had gone to the shrine of Zaynab. "Bahija Abdullah," said the old lady in Arnoun, "has gone to the shrine to pray for Ali's ruin. This woman will bring about his downfall." My grandmother

feared the prayers and the summons. A prayer in the shrine of Zaynab might be heard and answered. The skies, it was said, were opened at times. The petitioners and prayers—if warranted, if they came from a deeply felt wound—could be answered. The old lady in Arnoun and her former daughter-in-law believed in the same magic, in the same tales of retribution and vindication, and appealed to the same authorities. One prayed for Ali Ajami's ruin; one asked God to ward off evil, to bring her son back, well and triumphant.

The two women had contrasting styles of devotion. My grandmother was the more formalist of the two. She prayed regularly and on time. She prayed because such devotion came with the territory of her success. It was part of her self-esteem, of her duty. The world had been good to her. My mother was cavalier about prayer. She had ways of casting doubt on the piety of those who overdid their prayers. She acted as though she had a special line to the saintly imams. She who knew suffering could skip prayers and other religious observance yet still be counted among the chosen and the pious.

The formal acts of piety required a less hectic and a more settled life than my mother's. She expressed the skepticism of her world toward excessive piety with a favorite saying of hers: "If your neighbor made the pilgrimage to Mecca once, you have to watch him; if he goes twice, avoid his company; if he goes three times, move to another place." My mother said such things, I could see only with time, because the means for the pilgrimage were not available to her. She was not worried, she said. She trusted in the imams who mediated with God. There was, she was sure, an accounting system that struck from the record the pietistic deeds of those who had tormented others. She never worried, never had to worry, she said, about the pilgrimage of

her mother-in-law: Rawshna had been a strong-willed woman, a tyrant in her domain. She had given favors, and she had withheld them. All this would be in God's book, my mother was sure. Pilgrimage to Mecca was beyond my mother's means. It took more money than she could scrape together, more time than she could spend away from her sons and her work. Salvation, she believed, came to the sufferer who endured. God's design did not have to manifest itself today or tomorrow: dawn came after a long night. My mother was a long-distance runner.

The visit to the shrine deeply touched her. Soon after her return, inspired by what she had experienced, she brought the drama of Kerbala and the Shia heritage into our lives in a more direct way. She had made a *nidr* that my brother should take part in the annual Ashura celebrations on the tenth of the month of Muharram commemorating the martyrdom of Hussein. The *nidr* had been made a while back, when my brother's health had seemed to falter. The unfulfilled *nidr* troubled my mother, and she now wanted it redeemed. Her presence in the sanctuary of the saintly woman had reminded her of sacred duties.

Ashura was a celebration of sorrow—of mourners abandoning themselves to grief, of men beating themselves with chains. Nabatiyya was the center of the most elaborate celebrations. Every year, the Shia relived Kerbala and reenacted the tales of thirst. There were nine days of grief and wailing during which set pieces recalling the imams were read in the homes of the pious and of those who could afford to pay the reciters. The wailing and the sorrow reached its pitch on the tenth day—the actual day on which Imam Hussein had been martyred—in a Passion Play that recalled the tragedy of Kerbala.

Strict mullahs in Iran and in Lebanon, mullahs fastidious about the text and jealous over their prerogatives, had frowned on

the Passion Play, on the excesses of Ashura. But women like my mother and my grandmother ran afoul of the stern mullahs and interpreted the religion in their own way, by their own definitions of piety and devotion. The two women could say some choice words about mullahs and their ways, about the skeletons buried in the closets of the ones they knew, about the senility of the older clerics. The mullahs had their strict texts; the practicing believers had their rituals. So the month of Muharram of the Muslim year 1374—the year 1954 by the Christian calendar—found us in Arnoun for the days of reading and lamentation.

These were special days, days of suffering. A miserly brother of my grandmother's, one of the Alawiyyas, distributed some flour and some wheat to the needy. He even gave away some of the honey that came from his own beehives. He had always been careful with his honey. It was given on special occasions to those whose favors he needed, to those who had something to offer in return. But there was merit, religious merit, to be gained from charity on these sacred ten days. There was something of a believer in everyone, and my great-uncle had hedged his bets.

The readings at home were principally the activity of the women in the household. Our tradition said that for those who weep for what befell the Prophet's family God will ensure a "place of righteous mansions to dwell therein for countless years in Paradise." The weeping came more naturally to my mother than to my grandmother. There was merit in weeping. But there was a place, too, for the lady of the house, my grandmother, who retained the reciter, who fed the needy.

The work of men and of boys—the Passion Play—came only on the tenth day in Nabatiyya.

The Arnouni delegation was a small one. The men of the neighboring village of Yohmor taunted the Arnounis about the

contingent they had fielded for Ashura. Valor was not in the Arnounis, the people of Yohmor said. They knew the Arnounis as a timid lot from a "battle" the two villages had fought sometime back, a battle with sticks and stones that the poet-laureate of Yohmor had chronicled in a long poem that told how a small group of Yohmor's sons had put the people of Arnoun to flight.

My brother was among the boys in the white frocks chanting "*Ya Hassan, Ya Hussein*"—"Oh, Hassan, Oh Hussein"—after the second and third imams. It was a vivid scene, under a brilliant clear sky: my brother, a child of ten or eleven, in one hand holding a valued dagger given to him by my grandfather and, with the other hand, striking his head to the rhythmic chant. A razor cut had been made on my brother's head by a barber. The beating made the blood flow. I ran by my brother's side, an envious spectator, trying to keep up with the procession of mourners and frightening men with their long swords and chains—the men with white frocks soaking with blood.

The Passion Play itself was a thrilling drama. I knew the principal actors, the three Kuhail brothers from Nabatiyya. Two of them were teachers at my school in Beirut. But on this day, the brothers were the great personages they played: the venerable Imam Hussein, his younger half-brother and standard bearer, Abbas, who makes a brave excursion to the Euphrates to fetch water for the women and children, and his nephew, Kassem, who marries one of Imam Hussein's daughters before he falls to the archers of the ruler, Yazid. The Passion Play was staged in the center of Nabatiyya, in front of thousands of spectators in an open field by the market place, right in front of the town's largest mosque. The Kuhail brothers took their audience to the plain of Kerbala, in Iraq, and then on a journey to Damascus along with the caravan of orphans and widows and grieving sisters.

But we did not live in the Muslim year 1374. We lived by a "modern" calendar, in a city on the move, among a people intent on showing the outside world how far we all had traveled from the old rituals and the customs of our ancestors and our faith. My brother's deed was sanctioned in Arnoun. My grandmother had approved of it. My grandfather had not been enthusiastic about it, but he had offered no resistance. But there was furor over it among my aunts in West Beirut, women far younger, far more sophisticated than my mother. The deed done in Nabatiyya did not play well among the women of the city. The Passion Play, the procession of grief, the scenes with chains and daggers, were superstition, things of the past. We were busy discarding our village rituals as we went along. The land and the past were too close for comfort. We were within the gates of the city, scrambling for acceptance, anxious to scrub ourselves clean of the village ways.

When it was denounced as barbarism by women who were modern and à la mode, my brother reinterpreted the deed, saw it in a new and unflattering light. He returned to the city wearing a hat to cover the circle of a bruise around the wound left by the barber of Nabatiyya.

My mother accepted the judgment of my aunts. She accepted the division of things. She was of one world; her sons were on their way toward another. She learned to bend with the wind: this was her strength. My mother had built a cocoon for herself and for us. She was maintaining it with toil and patience. And I needed the warmth. It was my starting point. I had spent the early years of my childhood with a hidden terror that one day she would not be around. My father's sisters had teased me about the possibility of her marrying again, but I had never reasoned the thing out. My mother had always said that the world of men and of marriage was behind her, that she was content to live for my

brother and me. But I had known enough instability in my life—in Arnoun, in my father's house by the swamp, in my mother's room with the tin roof, in the world of my uncles and aunts in West Beirut—that I could not trust the ground I was standing on. I wanted the presence of my mother. And assured of her presence, I wanted to go beyond her world.

There were words of endearment that my mother knew—words that came from the land, words that mothers said to their sons. There were prayers to God and to his twelve imams to see wild boys through unpredictable times. There was Allah invoked every time a boy stepped outdoors or returned from an errand. I did not want to hear these words of endearment. They stood out in the city and flashed messages I did not want to see. Like her headscarf, which made me squirm at times, the words were words of villagers. My mother's affection smothered. And I was, as I always remained, her youngest. I was to be sheltered and protected. More affection than I wanted was mine to be had. The phobias and the fears were all around me. The summons and the prayers suffocated me; the "evil eye" trailed me at every turn.

My mother had mastered the language and skills of an old world: the coping with things one did not like, the waiting for dawn through a long night, the alternation between backbreaking toil and detours into consolation. The tradition which she inherited both sustained and crushed her. She believed in property but was without much property to her name. She believed that a woman lived through a man and derived her standing from his but was without a man. She had married two cruel men. She had been tormented by both. But she could, now and then, speak of the two marriages in consoling ways. The first husband had been a sayyid, a holy man, a descendant of the Prophet. As for the second husband, she saw him as a man with an "aura," a younger

man with good looks. For these marriages, for what had transpired, she had no apologies to make. Shame, she said, came from truly shameful things. She had married in accord with God's ways and the law of His Prophet. *Nasib*—fate, fortune—had decided the outcome of the two marriages.

And yet, my mother had a remarkable ability to remember the misfortune that had befallen her. I could not bear the retelling of the tales of hurt. What I needed was some oblivion. She lived with a permanent sense of siege. And I very desperately wanted to break out.

"My beloved mother, I do know of the hellish years you spent in my father's village, of the backbreaking toil. I know that my father's face reminds you of Imam Hussein's killer. It hurts me to no end to know what it was like, to think of how much you endured. I do regret those long walks of defeat between Arnoun and Nabatiyya. I do know that you spent a good deal of your life without a man's protection and a man's labor and a man's support, that you have more of the same to look forward to. Yes, you did tell me: I know that you once made the harsh trip between Arnoun and Nabatiyya under a fierce storm. I shall remember that I am a stepson, that my mother is not there to defend me against a heartless father. I know the tales of hurt you want me to remember. I live amidst the tales. All I want is for the tales to release me from their grip. If this is infidelity, so be it. I very much want to be your son, shall always be so. But I don't want to appropriate your sorrow and your defeat and make them mine. Surely in your galaxy of imams and their sayings, in your endless supply of parables and proverbs, there must exist the possibility of a life lived without man being hunter or prey."

Deep down, my mother may have concluded that her own rebellious spirit, a part of her that was quarrelsome and stubborn,

had been at work in her ruin. She taught, or tried to teach, lessons of quiet resistance. A saying of hers from the old culture said, in effect, that one ought to kiss the hand one could not break and ask God to break it. This was the wisdom of her world. That wisdom had come to her in the aftermath of two stormy marriages. But I did not want this for myself. The tradition—with its consolation, with its patience—came whole. It was like faith healing, in which one had to believe in the faith healer's art, in the cabalistic prescriptions, for the magic to work. Without that kind of belief, the magic was of no use.

We may have continued to kiss the hand of an elder—a grandfather, an older uncle, a father who required it—twice, of course, and then touch it to the forehead. But we were the first among our own people to look around before and after doing so, hoping that the deed was not witnessed by a friend, or by an Armenian boy whose team we had just humiliated on the soccer field a day or so ago, or by a girl we had been trying to impress. The rituals had been passed on to us—the rituals of peasants, of a well-ordered society. For the generation that preceded mine, the rituals made sense, sprang out of the earth, out of the way men and women lived and toiled. But it was different for us. The rituals were at once strident and pathetic. The great-uncle insisting on his hand being kissed twice was now demanding it to assert his threatened sense of domination and precedence. And the boy submitting to it was well on his way toward viewing the man with the red fez as an embarrassing relic of the past.

When the sons of mothers with headscarves and stern fathers who barely knew how to smile began the scramble out of the shadow of their elders, we would trip over one another. It would not be a solitary passage.

The movies of a foreign world were coming into our midst. The Western infected a whole generation with an American bug—the thrill of open spaces, of adventure. The posters of the movie house in our neighborhood were pure works of seduction: Jane Russell in *Montana Belle*, Rhonda Fleming, Virginia Mayo in *Colorado Territory*. The wind blew one of Jane Russell's posters off a billboard. A lucky boy picked it up, hung it in his home. This was the alleyway's first pinup.

The films came our way a few years after they had been released in the land where they were made. We were becoming a dumping ground for movies. The Western may have been past its prime in America, but it reigned in our midst. In America, the movies were entertainment. For us, the line between the adventure on the screen and the land over there, the country that made them, was blurred. We knew so little of the distant land that we took its films for its reality. We saw America through the Western. We fell for the films and for the country that was turning them out. Posse, gunslingers, drifters, prairies, cowhands—even the words seemed so magical, so wondrous to me.

I had seen a fair number of Egyptian films when I sat for my first American film. The movies of the distant land made the Egyptian films look like a shabby affair. Entertaining as they were, Egyptian films were about a world somewhat similar to ours. In the Egyptian films, women said that they had just given a man they had succumbed to "the most precious thing" they had. Daughters were lectured that a girl's honor was like a match that could only be lit once. Sons feared their father. Everyone worried what their neighbors thought of them. There were squabbles over

small plots of land. I knew all too well about these squabbles: such squabbles were the stuff of our lives.

It took no time for us to develop our own taste and heroes. We all loved Audie Murphy. We had no taste for John Wayne or his style. Perhaps he was a bit too tall, too slow in our eyes. We all preferred the shorter, more intense, more boyish Audie Murphy. And we rooted for Alan Ladd in *Shane*. (A definite bias in favor of the shorter heroes.) We loved to hate Jack Elam, the perennial bad guy with his villainous looks and his unseeing left eye. We were appalled, we felt nearly violated, if he laid his hands on Dorothy Malone.

The first American film I sat for may have been *Ride the High Country*, starring Randolph Scott. I saw countless films of Scott, who starred in many Westerns in the 1940s but became big among the boys of our neighborhood a few years later, in the early 1950s, when his movies reached us. But it was *High Noon*, not a film starring Scott, that was the perfect film for me. Everything came together in *High Noon*, it seemed. It was a stark film, the quintessential tale of a loner, blessed with a simple, unforgettable title.

The tension of the story unfolding in a single day—Sheriff Will Kane making a run for it out of Hadleyville to escape the wrath of a dangerous killer who has come to settle a score with him for "sending him up" and then Kane pulling up on the open prairie and returning to take on the killer and his gang, even though the good citizens of Hadleyville have deserted the lawman in his hour of need—and the haunting melody of Tex Ritter's "Do Not Forsake Me, Oh My Darlin'" gave *High Noon* an appeal other films could not match.

The country turning out the Westerns was implanting itself, and its ways and pop culture, under the skin of people in

remote places. No other culture had made itself so accessible to people beyond its shores. No other culture had ever traveled with such ease. We could not possess the culture of France: that had been claimed by the Christians of the country whose traffic with France went back centuries. To speak French you had to speak it right—speak it *comme il faut*—and we could not. The Christians of the East loved France: *Al Umm Hasun*, it was called—Our Beloved Mother. We could not be parties to that romance. Nor had we around us the ways and manners of the British rulers of Palestine and Jordan and Iraq. What was around, what had burst into our midst, were the ways of America, carried here by her missionaries and schools and, more decisively for us, by her films. The American film was unlike anything I had been exposed to before. Once I acquired the taste, I grew addicted.

Two friends of mine were my steady companions to the movie theaters in our neighborhood. I had to hustle my mother for the price of admission. Movies had not been part of her life. She had never seen an Arabic-speaking Egyptian film, let alone a foreign one. She had doubts about the movies. Movies were a strange innovation that played with the mind; movies were bad for the eyes. But she was helpless against a particular argument of mine: American movies, I claimed, were good for learning English and, thus, good for passing examinations. This said, she reached to where she always kept her money—in a white handkerchief tied to the strap of her bra—and gave what I needed.

Sometimes I was able to see a whole film right from the beginning, to be there for the previews of coming attractions and for the cartoons, to join in the thunderous applause that greeted MGM's lion. More often, because I went so often and had to stretch what money I had, I waited outside for twenty or thirty minutes to get in through a special deal with the movie attendant,

who ran a side-business after the ticket window closed, a way of picking up some cash for himself.

One of my friends was a neighbor of the movie attendant. Most of the time he was admitted free of charge. And he was always admitted ten or fifteen minutes before me and our other friend. As was his habit, he insisted that the scenes we missed were the most exquisite. It was when we were outside pleading with the man at the door, pacing the floor, that Rhonda Fleming had been most alluring, that a steamy episode had taken place between Jane Russell and the outlaw, that the buttons on Dorothy Malone's tight shirt had snapped, or that Randolph Scott was most authoritative in dispatching one of his challengers.

Movies of rebellious American teenagers were also coming our way. If the guardians of morality, the attentive gatekeepers of our country had known, they would have banned such films. In a distant land, so the films suggested, teenagers did not kiss the hands of their elders. We were a receptive audience for these films of rebellion, invariably on the side of those hacking away at the rules and at those who enforced the rules. We sympathized when rebellion ended in self-destruction. We knew about James Dean, about his tragic death, before his films reached us, and we were ready for him when the films finally made their way to our movie theaters. We loved the style, the intensity, and the anger. We loved the turned-up collar.

When I first started with American films, I had relied on the Arabic subtitles. But soon, like a beginner trying to master a bicycle who gets that thrilling sensation that he is on his own, that no one is helping him stay up there, I realized that I could ignore the subtitles and enter directly into the character's universe. It was a heady thing, and it gave me a sense of being set apart from the less fortunate. From the films I picked up favorite phrases and

words. I loved to say "OK" to things that were OK and to things that were not. I loved the sound of it, the free determination of its meaning. "See you later" was another favorite expression.

The American films helped me break the monopoly of my English teachers at the National School on the glamorous new language. As taught by my teachers, English had been an extension of an old sensibility. It was taught the same way all other subjects were taught. It was made prohibitive, difficult, stilted. Its reference was to fixed objects. "This is a chair; this is a book. This is my chair; this is my book." We had chanted the words the same way we had chanted our Arabic lessons.

There were two choices for the elementary examinations conducted by the Ministry of Education: dictation for those choosing English, *dictée* for those choosing French. *Dictée* was what the boys on the other side of the line, in Christian Beirut, were good at. The Muslims opted for English. One half of the country, it seemed, had continued to partake of the language of the former French masters of the country. The other half of the country had embraced English—the language of the United States, the new power on the horizon. English had come to impoverished schools like mine through Palestinian teachers who had learned it from the British rulers of Palestine. In exile, the Palestinians worked without permits, accepted low wages. They took what little payment was offered them; they taught what little English they knew.

School English and spoken English remained different things for me for some time. It was only a few years later that I bridged the gap and written English acquired life, became bearable, and connected with the world.

My schooling, the schooling of my generation and my peers, could not have communicated the wonder, the freedom of a foreign language. My schooling had not given me an appreciation

of the material I was reading. Classical, written Arabic itself had been transmitted to us in a forbidding, stilted way. No one taught the enjoyment of reading. No teacher bothered to explain the meaning of what was read: it was formal Arabic text, read for the grammar and, of course, for Arabic composition. It was known—how could it be forgotten?—that composition was essential to passing the examinations administered by the state. We were taught composition the way we were taught everything else: the rules, the prohibitions, the formal structure. The "three-legged" essay—an introduction, a subject, a conclusion—set the form of our prose; we were to be its obedient transmitters.

The personal voice was muted in the compositions. It couldn't emerge. It was alien to the culture. The writer's feelings and judgments were not what the endeavor was about. A skill had been passed on, and the skill had to be displayed on command. There were set ways of describing nature: we described cedars we had never seen, mountains we had never laid eyes on. There were fixed, worn-out ways of describing the books we read. Likewise, our books and our songs said that we had such a beautiful country, but we hardly noticed. We walked past things: our people were worried about the eyes and the judgments. A daughter-in-law was far too worried about her mother-in-law to take notice of the lily at the foot of the olive tree in the village. My Uncle Ahmad carried far too great a share of the family's burden to take in the perfume of the orange blossoms. My mother was too busy, too fixated on the past, to take notice of the snow-covered ridge of Mount Hermon, not far from the cliffs of Arnoun, or to savor the coming of spring. The spring had to battle with the ghosts and with the eyes, and the spring lost. So many seasons of spring lost out to the eyes and to the judgments.

It could not have occurred to those who transmitted knowledge to ask us to describe the things we saw, bumped into, maneuvered our way around—the crooked alleyways, the open sewers, the tin shacks. Instead, there were examples of Arabic composition and pieces of poetry that came from as remote a world as the Arabian Desert. In the poems from the desert, it was standard for the poet to come upon the abandoned site of the tribe of his beloved. We were in the city; that experience was not ours. The sites and the themes of the poetry were not ours. We just plugged into them. And the words never really came to life. The classical poet may have said that the eyes of his beloved were as beautiful as those of a cow. In Beirut of the 1950s, this couldn't have taken any romance too far. But that was what we were taught.

The works of history that could have awakened the mind and the senses, moved the language around and given it life, were hopeless as well. These works paraded names of kings, fixed dates of battles and of conquests. What little history was taught put our small country at the center of the world. Our Phoenician ancestors, the history books taught, had invented the alphabet, had taken the olive tree to Greece. Phoenician ships once sailed every sea. The Phoenician city of Sidon had nurtured her daughter, the city of Tyre. Together, the two cities had been thriving entities. It was said in the books that Alexander the Great had had a hard time tearing himself away from the beauty of Sidon. I had passed through Sidon and Tyre. To get to our ancestral village we climbed upward, through the seaside town of Damour and its banana orchards, then, before reaching the treacherous, twisting road through the rocky hills, through Sidon. The cities of the texts were grander than the tumbled towns languishing on the coast.

The ways of the coast—softened by commerce and the sea—were not ours. The Phoenician seafarers could not be embraced

and understood, or turned into one's own. The history of Lebanon of the last three centuries was the history of the Mount Lebanon range—the heartland of the country where Maronites and Druze lived. They had ruled Mount Lebanon, divided it, warred over it. It was the psychology of the mountain and its tangled relationship with Mediterranean commerce and politics that shaped Lebanon and gave it its identity and myths. A boy like myself from the village of the hinterland could find little of himself or of his people in the history presented him. Face to face with the history of Mount Lebanon—its princes, its celebrated inaccessibility, its traffic with France and Europe—it was easy to see that the remote hinterland of my people was an appendage of the country.

I learned that Lebanon was the "cradle of civilizations," that it was mentioned in the Bible seventy-five times. I learned that mighty empires had warred over my country. These bits of learning were like incantations. Everywhere around us were the monuments of nations that came our way. The two castles of Sidon—the castle of the sea and the castle on land—were built by the Crusaders. And of course there had always been the castle in the village, Beaufort, and all the history it evoked. We took in all the invaders and the passersby. Those magnificent tall columns in the town of Baalbak, in the eastern part of the country, were Roman monuments. The town of Baalbak itself was poor—a place where hashish growers and smugglers lived beyond the law, a place of tribal feuds and vendettas. It was a place beyond attention. But once a year, there was an extravagant festival: the smart set poured into the town, floodlights lit up the magnificent columns, folkloric dancers celebrated the country's spirit. It was one of those sights for the postcards.

"And, yes, pupils, there are Christians and Muslims in Lebanon. Christians and Muslims share this beloved country,

are lucky to be sons of the same land. The finicky Sunni Muslims of the coastal cities of Lebanon—Beirut, Sidon, Tripoli—and the Shia Muslims whom they loathe are all Lebanese. And there are fierce Druze mountaineers up there in the Chouf Mountains who believe in the transmigration of souls, who believe that pious souls migrate to China, who wear baggy trousers, brightly colored sashes, and tall felt hats. Bearers of an esoteric eleventh century faith known only to the initiated among them, living in a sort of no-man's land between Christians and Muslims, the Druze are men of pride and circumspection. The mysteries of the Druze faith are to be protected. Druze who break the code and let others into the mysteries of their religion could be punished by death. "Death without mercy," the code teaches. The founder of the Druze sect taught them subtlety too: "Follow every action stronger than mine and guard me in your heart." The Druze were once feudal lords, the terror of the country. But the superior numbers of the Christians and the newfangled skills of a world of traders had forced them into a shell. But they, too, the Druze, are Lebanese.

"On a plateau overlooking the coastal town of Jounieh, there is a large, imposing white statue of the Virgin, the statue of Sitt al Harissa, the Lady of the Guard. The statue has the protective Virgin looking to the Mediterranean. (The sea has always been of great importance to the Maronites: across the sea is the Christian world of the West.) Within the dramatic mountain range in whose gorges and valleys the Maronite towns and villages are nestled is a world unto itself, with chapels and convents and red-tiled roofs shimmering in the sun. Insular men these Maronites. They seem to keep to themselves. They trace their history to a seventh-century monk who brought them from the plains of Syria to these forbidding mountains to practice their independent faith.

"When the Crusaders came, the fierce Maronite mountaineers came down from the mountain to greet the invaders, bearing gifts of food, welcoming them as brothers in the faith. They even guided the invaders on their march to Jerusalem. The Latin Kingdom set up by the Crusaders, in the eyes of the Muslims a deed of violation, was for the Maronites an affair of triumphant Christianity. Centuries ago, the Maronites entered into union with the Catholic church in Rome. But even the Holy See could not subdue their independent spirit. They remained clannish and stubborn. On *Id al Salib*, the Feast of the Cross, the bonfires atop the Maronite Mountain are lit in memory of St. Helena. These bonfires tell of a people determined to keep at bay the world in the plains below—a people who live at the edge of massacre. This is the way the Maronites have seen their history and their situation. The massacres of the midnineteenth century that pitted Druze against Maronite—massacres that men and women speak of as though they were events of a cruelly remembered day sometime last week—were caused by Englishmen who sponsored the Druze, by meddlesome Frenchmen who were the protectors of the Christians, and, of course, by scheming Maronites who pleaded for help from French brothers of the faith. But this fragile republic of ours is to live with all these memories and to look past them. Overlook the fact that the Maronites think of themselves as part of the *La Mission Civilisatrice* of France, and that they look down on the multitude with whom they share this country. They may at times act as though they are shipwrecked in this part of the world, away from the Western world with which they identify. But, they, too, are Lebanese.

"Dear Pupils, the Crescent and the Cross embraced in Lebanon; the few massacres along the way were the intrigues of outsiders. Left alone, our land was a veritable paradise. Trouble

came, trouble erupted, when strangers disrupted the peace of the land, played us off against one another."

Mothers told a different truth than the official history. The truth that boys took in with their mothers' milk dispensed with official cant. Mothers, my own included, said that Christians were *najas*, impure. "Eat at a Druze's, sleep at a Christian's," said the mothers. It was a saying intended as a warning to those who would trust the Druze. The Druze, the fierce and cunning Druze, killed and slit throats. Better risk an impure meal at a Christian's home than risk death at the hands of a Druze. The deadly phobias and the official banalities were side by side. The history was blatantly defective. Imagination had to be awakened by a different material, the written word had to come together with the world of familiar things. The written word had to be "softened" and believed.

IV

―――◦◉◦―――

> I don't know what would have become of me if
> I had not been a reading boy. I suppose that in a
> futile, childish way I would have gone crazy. But
> I was a reading boy...I read! What did not I read?

The words are Joseph Conrad's. They recall a difficult child-hood in Poland: a childhood of loss, then of exile. It was with the books and magazines my younger aunts read that I began to read. Two of my aunts were trying, to the extent they were permitted by the family, by custom, by scarcity, to be young women of the city. One of them was a bright secondary school teacher. The other, my Aunt Zaynab, the youngest, was herself in secondary school. She couldn't have been more than six or seven years older than me. She loved romantic novels. She read them in secret. For added protection, she removed the covers. Romantic novels with suggestive covers were forbidden. They were as for-bidden as loitering on the balcony, as idling too long in front of

a mirror, as moving about when adults talked or quarreled. The literacy of women was a subversive thing. Books were windows that brought in all kinds of storms and troubles. The schooling of women had been forced onto reluctant families, like ours, by an ungiving land. A schooled woman who taught brought a salary home at the end of every month, as one of my aunts did. But the fear of what literacy brought in its train remained.

Novels got on my Uncle Ahmad's nerves. They did so because they were unreal, because they were "made up," because some scoundrel had spun them out and pocketed other people's money. "We should all do such a thing, were life so easy for all of us as it is for these sons of whores making up these episodes." He lifted one of the novels—its leading character's name may have been Midhat. "Where is this Midhat? Does anyone know him? Has anyone met him? Why do we have to go on reading about him?" The novel with Midhat as its principal character was torn to shreds.

Like my youngest aunt, I had to learn where to find these censored books and where to hide them when my Uncle Ahmad turned up. Like her, I became a devoted reader of an Egyptian women's magazine called *Hawa*, or *Eve*. I read and reread the letters sent to *Hawa* by some of its readers about silent, unconsummated love affairs, conceived on Cairo's balconies. My youngest aunt and her cousin Nadia, a daring and *avant-garde* young woman of Beirut, followed the romance of a young, handsome, curly-haired Egyptian actor named Omar Sharif and the leading star of the Egyptian cinema of the time, the demure Faten Hamama. Like them, I became obsessed with the gossip about Sharif and Faten. Faten, a relatively small woman with a breathless voice and languid looks, was unattainable, or so all her movies made her out to be. Faten Hamama was an enticing

mix of the virginal and the suggestive. Men who played opposite her ached to get her, to get close to her. But she always escaped unblemished and unclaimed, still prepared to give herself only in marriage. Faten had two or three rivals whose parts involved dancing or drinking with a rich pursuer before slipping into his unfurnished apartment. There were other parts played by flirtatious women who got themselves in trouble, who went down at dusk in the villages of the Nile Delta to meet the local landlord, offering just enough resistance to make it interesting. But Faten was made of purer material. And thus when Omar Sharif came along, it was a love affair.

I read Khalil Gibran. He was special to my countrymen and to my generation, part of the country's distinction: a tormented boy in Lebanon, at eleven he had gone to America with his mother and siblings to escape his tyrannical father, settling in Boston before beginning his work in New York City. He might have been the first serious writer I was introduced to. He had written of the Lebanon he knew as a child—the Maronite Mountain, the monasteries with their stern priests who often betrayed their trust and catered to the mighty, the heartless landlords, the tormented men and women who had to make their way past scarcity and custom and terror. I did not know the monasteries when I began reading Gibran. It must have been six or seven years later when I first ventured into the well-kept grounds of a solitary, imposing monastery in the hills beyond Sidon. I had not previously seen the part of the country where Gibran was born. But I had no difficulty entering into Gibran's world.

The first piece by Gibran I read was a short story entitled "Yuhanna the Madman." It was about a young shepherd who loved the open fields and who read the Bible in secret because the priests never wanted simple-minded men to know the real

teachings of Jesus. In the story, Yuhanna's calves wander onto the vast grazing grounds of the monastery; when he follows, Yuhanna is seized by the monks and begs to be released. What gives the story its special quality are Yuhanna's words—the simple shepherd observing "power in its velvets and satins" and "misery in its rags and tatters." On one side, Yuhanna saw harsh "tyranny," on the other blind obedience. "Which one is parent to the other? Is tyranny a strong tree that grows not except on low ground?"

I read more of Gibran, for the sound of his words, for the sensibility. The bulk of his work behind me, I went straight to Egyptian fiction. I wanted more plot than Gibran's short stories had to offer.

It turned out I had stepped into Egyptian literature at an appropriate time. The novels were becoming more experimental, more daring, more interested in the lives of ordinary men and women. When I began reading I started out with one old gentleman, Mustapha al Manfaluti, who wrote unabashed tearjerkers—stories of lovers dying at the same time for no reason other than forced separation decreed by a heartless parent. Manfaluti had grown up in the latter part of the nineteenth century. His world was not mine. I had had no standard of judgment when I started reading him. All I knew was that he was an improvement on the textbooks at school. But the younger breed of Egyptian writers soon made Manfaluti *passé*. Teenagers stopped reading him; or at least they never admitted it if they did.

The new Egyptian writers, writers like Ihsan Abdul Qaddus and Yusuf Sibai, experimental, daring souls who played with the language, who softened the written text and wrote romantic novels in which young readers could recognize themselves and their yearnings, brought Cairo and its people to life. In the novels, lovers strolled by the Nile at dusk. In no time, the boulevards

and cafés along the Nile had become familiar territory that I could conjure up with no great difficulty. Wealthy characters in the novels led young impressionable women astray, took them to "furnished apartments" in the posh district of Zamalek and seduced them. And Zamalek, too, with its lavish apartments and gullible young women was becoming a familiar place.

The chatter of Egypt was the chatter of a more genteel, more settled, society than ours in Lebanon. I became fond of the place—of its banter, of its humor, of its tame countryside, of the way its coquettes ensnared and eluded the men who pursued them. There was Groppi, a Cairo café with a foreign name, where the characters in the novels always met. Everybody eventually found their way there. I, too, wanted to drop in at Groppi. (Years later, when I finally made it to Cairo, Groppi, now seedy and rundown, though still staffed, as in the novels, by black Sudanese waiters, nearly broke my heart.)

The Egyptian novels were beginning to teach me how to write a more independent kind of Arabic than my teachers and textbooks had inflicted upon me. Soon, I was trying my hand at pieces of writing of my own. When I began finding my way into small corners in my grandfather's home with a book in my hand, ignoring visiting cousins and relatives, my addiction to the books and the magazines struck my father's family as odd and objectionable. But the objections subsided. I was beginning to show some skill at writing letters. And in a country where families were losing sons and daughters to distant places, where the elders were still largely illiterate, writing good letters was no small matter.

Egyptian fiction had taken me beyond the world of my childhood. It had seen me through many a family squabble over land, over money, over slights, over mysterious obsessions that seemed to get hold of men and women and throw them into vendettas and

feuds that lent themselves to no conceivable resolution. The books made my Uncle Ahmad's outbursts more bearable. Engrossed in the books, I could always block him out. When I meandered out of the books, I could plug into timeless conversations and disputes. There was Ahmad lecturing the younger women not to cross their legs, not to speak too loudly or too quietly, or just wondering to himself as to what desperate ill-starred man was going to marry one of the younger women at home. My Aunt Sakiba worried whether appearances could be kept, whether money could be scraped together for new furniture for the drawing room, for new shoes for my younger aunts. There were complaints that no one in this neighborhood extended invitations. The tobacco crop always fell short of the hopes pinned on it, and the tobacco monopoly was again late in making the payment for this year's crop. There was a snob in the distant family, a lady with new money, with fastidious manners. Everyone wondered why she should put on airs and whether she had forgotten her years of trial and poverty. She was still a peasant, it was said of the snob: she could never quite master the ways of the city.

Stepping out of the Paris sewer, out of Jean Valjean's world, I would catch the hushed rendition of a story about a neighboring woman or a relative who was in trouble with her husband. The wife had struck back: she had mixed her urine or the blood of her menstrual cycle with the food of the faithless husband. Now the husband, under his wife's spell, had forgotten the madness. Assured of the triumph of the resourceful wife, I could plunge back into the sewer and rejoin Jean Valjean as he carries unconscious Marius to safety, gasping for fresh air from the vent-holes.

—⟋⟍—

I must have had my nose in a book when Sakna, one of the younger of the four unmarried aunts, was married off to a Lebanese who had returned from Sierra Leone to marry a woman from the old land. Had he had his way, this was the kind of marriage my Uncle Ahmad foresaw for all his unmarried sisters. My grandfather had frowned on the marriage. But Ahmad had been persistent. The young woman, barely sixteen years of age, was not good at school. Besides, she was very pretty, with long hair, a full figure, the fair skin of her mother. As my people said, it was safer for this one, who might have been a flirt, to go for an early marriage, to walk out of the home of her father into the home of her husband. No fool, Ahmad knew his sister. He held out to her an appealing prospect: The schooling she disliked would come to an end, there would be money, unimaginable amounts of it, money for fancy tailors and for summer rentals in the pretty hill towns overlooking Beirut, and there would be the freedom of her own domain. She could rule the roost, he assured her; the smitten suitor, a man deep in middle age, would give her everything she wanted. Sakna went along.

The man she married had gone to West Africa, from one of the larger towns in our part of the country, as a young man. He had no extended clan to claim him. He dwelt on the details of his passage from the country; they were his tale of hurt and redemption. His mother had died when he was a child. Growing up, he was hounded by a cruel stepmother and a heartless father. To his village came tales of money made in faraway Africa. Once he caught the bug, he became restless. His life in the village became unbearable. He wanted to leave for Africa. His father obliged and provided the fare for the passage. His first destination was Dakar. The ship's first port

of call was Marseilles. Then came a voyage of two weeks. Aboard the ship, long days must have been given over to fantasies of the great wealth that awaited him among the Africans, to dreams of revenge against those who had slighted and tormented him as a child. He no doubt looked into the future and saw his father, an old and bent man, welcoming him back, blessing his success. It had to be so for him: that was the way our country banished its sons and continued to hold them at the same time.

But Dakar turned out to be a dissolute town, poorer than the land he left behind. And soon the French who ruled Dakar called the young Lebanese villager to military service. He had not come that far, though, to fight the wars of the French; he had his own wars, his own accounts to settle. He quickly departed to Sierra Leone, then a British preserve.

Arriving in Sierra Leone, the young villager joined a growing Lebanese presence of other men with stories and dreams like his own. The first wave of immigrants, so the legend of the Lebanese had it, had made their way to Sierra Leone in the early years of this century. The "pioneers" had gone there by accident. New York or Boston had been their intended destination. But they had paid their fees to unscrupulous agents. After their first stop in Marseilles, they found out that they did not have enough money for a passage to the New World, that they lacked the proper health forms. They had a choice to make: they could go back to Lebanon or head off to West Africa. They knew this of West Africa: it had not been the object of their dreams. But it was an easy call to make. They knew the harshness of their old country, the difficulty of going back and facing their families with empty hands. They knew that the gangplank to the ship, once raised, snapped their link to their old world. They knew the terms of the farewell on the docks of Beirut: they were to return as triumphant men loaded

with wealth or run and hide somewhere in God's country. They headed off to Sierra Leone.

The Lebanese followed the railroad deep into the bush. The Creoles wanted the Lebanese traders out of the way, railed against them to the colonial power as parasites and vagabonds who brought no new skills to the colony, who kept to themselves and their own. The Creoles had not wavered in their opposition to the Lebanese. But our people were not easily deterred. I read in a book that they were immune to sun and fever. They would carve out a role for themselves.

In Sierra Leone, the young villager had done the sort of work that others of his kind did. The Lebanese had begun as hawkers, wholesalers of rice, of kola nuts, in remote places where European traders had not bothered to go. They went about the streets of Freetown—the colonial city put up by the British on the coast—with boards strapped around their necks selling razors, combs, coral beads. It was by the cheap coral beads made of celluloid that the Creoles of the African Coast named the Lebanese. The Lebanese, "the Corals," were intruding on their trading turf. But the Creoles could not know what demons drove our people. The Lebanese went deeper into the interior of the country. They became middlemen between the African farmers and the banks. They did well by the commerce and the traffic that the two world wars had brought to the coastal towns of Africa. By the mid 1950s, when the diamond rush began in the country, the Africans and the Lebanese were breaking into the business that for twenty years had been a British monopoly. Thousands of African miners searched for diamonds. The Lebanese, like my two aunts and their husbands, were traders.

So far away, we lived under the spell of those diamond fields of Sierra Leone, those alluvial diamonds that had been first

discovered in the Gboboro stream of the Kano district. In Sierra Leone, we believed, diamonds grew on trees. Even the clumsiest soul could go there, trick the native Africans, give them an umbrella or a pair of shoes for a diamond that would set the world right in Lebanon. The mines of Sierra Leone had become a mythic world, our own El Dorado.

And fittingly enough for this mythical land, we were to learn that the romance and the cruelty and the heartbreak were rolled together. For every bit of news about one trader with wits and guile and a stroke of luck there would come our way an endless stream of grief—near-brushes with success, tales of defeat and thwarted expeditions. We all said how deeply we had loved our land. But the deepest terror in the years to come was the terror of being deported from Sierra Leone, sent back to face the eyes and the judgment of the ones who stayed behind and who waited.

My Aunt Sakna departed for Africa with her husband immediately after their marriage. The diamond trade beckoned. With luck, one diamond deal could realize their dreams. Men in my country who went off to Africa usually left their wives at home in Lebanon. They went off to make money and left the women to wait, to keep the world intact. But my aunts were ambitious and restless women. They made their way to Africa to open shops, to help deal with the native miners who turned up with diamonds to sell. My Aunt Sakna must have been happy to leave behind my Uncle Ahmad's boot camp—the tight discipline, the harshness. She didn't know what lay in store for her.

My first exposure to Beirut's airport—what was then a large hangar, really—was when we all bade her farewell. We all knew why she had to go, this young woman on an uncertain passage to a faraway place. My grandmother—a woman with strong nerves—was overcome with grief as pretty young Sakna boarded

the plane. It was known in those quiet ways in which we, the youngsters, knew such things that my grandmother had opposed the marriage—the separation from her daughter that it promised, the age of Sakna's husband. But my grandfather had prevailed. This was Sakna's way out and her lot. The promise of wealth and independence, of a world of her own, were her compensation for a marriage to an older man.

Soon my Uncle Abbas, then a young man in his midtwenties, at a dead end in Lebanon, no longer the head of the National School, followed his sisters and his brothers-in-law to Sierra Leone. He knew next to nothing of the land to which he was departing other than the fragments supplied by the Lebanese expatriates who had come back from Sierra Leone. He knew what I knew; we had listened to the same tales. We both knew that there was a street in Freetown called "Wata Street"—or Water Street, as I learned on my own—where Lebanese had their shops. But beyond the subject of their shops our relatives and kinsmen in Sierra Leone never ventured. They knew only a few words of pidgin English. Nothing was said of the colonial town decaying on the beach, of the Creoles learning the ways of the white rulers, of the governor general and his garden parties, of the British colonial officials in the smart bungalows in the hills overlooking the city. (That was one from Graham Greene's *Travels with My Aunt*. Greene was remarkable in his depiction. I went to him years later, and there in book form in *The Heart of the Matter* and *Journey Without Maps* I found this world laid bare.) Nothing was said about the quarrels of the "Syrians," as they were known, about the diamond fever that seized them all.

The Africa of our imaginations was a lucky land—a land of diamonds and opportunity. It was also a place of sensual fulfillment. In the years of my boyhood, when my family was beginning

to see its men and women off to Africa, there were hushed tales of a place that had a world with different, more permissive ways. A relative sent back a postcard of a bare-breasted African woman. The postcard played with our imagination. I never knew if such photos had played with my Uncle Abbas's imagination.

We knew—through the women who spoke of it, the men who boasted of it—that they had had their African women. The life of the senses alongside the shops and the hawking of the beads and the running of the diamonds. My aunt's husband had had a daughter born out of wedlock to an African mother. Nothing had been said of the young daughter until she turned up years later, a large and full-figured woman, vibrant and brown-skinned: the mulatta daughter of his youth in Africa alongside his white young wife.

A boy some sixteen or seventeen years of age, a distant relative, returned from Sierra Leone during this same period. I must have been little more than twelve years then. He came for the summer. He told of sexual exploits with the bare-breasted women. "Nothing to it," he said. "It is all there and no brothers or father come after you as they would in Lebanon."

There was something else about him that made him seem glamored to me. He had gone to a faraway place. Books had transported me to distant places and times. I knew the Africa of books and movies—and postcards. The thick African forests versus the stark earth of Lebanon. Had one of my aunts taken me along at the time, as some young boys were taken to labor in the batik shops, I would have jumped at the opportunity. But I was a "schoolboy." Africa was for those who had given up on the dream of schooling.

Now that I was skilled at letter writing, my relatives had me compile their sonorous sentences in their letters. The letters had

their structure, their set form, their hints dictated to me. And after one or two years of this, I could almost tune out the person dictating the letter and still get the message across: "The children are fine, the school tuition is due, we all yearn to see your face and pray for your return. The *Eid al Fitr* [the festival following the month of Ramadan, the month of fasting] is approaching. And the *Eid al Fitr* has expenses—shoes for the children, new clothes, some spending money for the amusement park. No, don't believe the gossip you hear: everyone is in good health, praying to protect you from the evil eye and the schemes of the ill-wishers. Your father says make sure you are 'a man,' that you build a house in the village when you return, that you show your rivals your spine and your skill."

Letters had to be read from the traders writing back from Liberia and Sierra Leone or from the Ivory Coast (another romantic name conjuring up the forest and expanses and the wildlife of Africa): "I received your letters and your gift of seeds and sweets, the pictures of the children. I came close to the diamond deal of a lifetime. But the malicious ill-wishers informed on me. I was lucky to escape being deported. What little I had saved had to grease the palms of the authorities here to let me stay. But I will try again. Please tell everyone that money does not grow on trees in Africa, that I am wasting the tender years of my life here. The money is earned with the sweat of the brow. Keep the children studying. I don't want to hear anything but the best about all of you. Yes, I will think about buying a piece of land in Beirut; I know that the price of land is going through the roof. You tell me that a relative made a fortune out of one piece of land. Don't believe him; he always had a vivid imagination, that Nabil. Remember, he is the one who used to come back from the open fields of the village with tales of snakes that he had captured and

domesticated, with tales of an encounter with a pack of wolves; he is the one who claimed that he once outwitted the hyena in the early hours of dawn, acted dazed as though he had fallen under the spell of the creature, followed it to the cave where it had devoured its previous victim, and then made a run for it by leaving his jacket behind for the hyena to tear at."

No letter I read from Sierra Leone—or Monrovia—communicated any curiosity for the landscape or the culture. Like in the tales from the Lebanese who had returned, there was no word about the life of Sierra Leone. It could have been that my relatives were not trained to look; it could have been their elemental racialism, their distance from the Africans. Perhaps the wounds inflicted by the old country ran too deep; perhaps the ghosts were too powerful. These were people bent on returning. They told of things that glamored them, added to them: it was all part of what had fallen to them in the world of African forests and clearings, in the country up river. But the places remained blank; what mattered were the comings and goings of the Lebanese. Of Freetown, hardly a word was said by the men dispatching letters to the old country. Our people sleepwalked through foreign places.

—〰—

A distant fight between the Algerians and the French helped bring me to my grandfather's attention in a serious way. His hopes for me—for a life of learning, as he understood it—took shape after I had spoken at a rally my school held in support of the Algerian struggle against the French. The year must have been 1957, when I was twelve years of age. I knew very little then of the fight between the Algerians and the French. When revolution had broken out in Algeria in 1954, it had seemed a distant fight. But

new politics were coming our way. Money was being donated for the Algerians. A tin box was set aside in my school for collecting contributions.

I read an impassioned poem some nameless poet had written about Algeria. It was addressed by a fighter in Algeria's mountains to his beloved woman. The romance and the politics came together for me. I read the poem with conviction. This was still a time when the passion of nationalism was real, when its promise was believed.

My grandfather knew very little about Algeria and the Algerians. But it was enough that they were a Muslim population fighting against the *Franjis*. My grandfather had seen the French come into his world after the Great War, and he had seen them pack up and leave. As rulers go, the French may not have been such a bad lot. They had given the Shia a break; they had recognized Shia courts. The infidels, the *Franjis*, had been fairer to the Shia than the Ottoman Turks who were Sunni Muslims and who saw themselves as the "sword of Islam." It was the French who, in 1920, had come up with the idea of *Grand Liban*, Greater Lebanon, and made South Lebanon part of a larger republic. But my grandfather had remained indifferent to the world beyond his village and his land. It was from my grandfather that I had learned a couplet that came from the interwar years:

> Ya Franca Hiddi wa Irahli
> Ijaky Hitler Abu Ali
> Oh France, dismantle and depart
> On your trail is Hitler, Abu Ali

Abu Ali, the name given Hitler, was a name of endearment given to lovable little thugs, to village and neighborhood rogues. The war was turned into something familiar—something like

the battle once fought between the village of Arnoun and the neighboring village of Yahmur.

What mattered to my grandfather was that I, his grandson, had stood up in a gathering and had read a long poem. The poem could have been about the tobacco crop; it could have been a relative's eulogy. My grandfather loved the worlds of politics, of books, of classical Arabic. The reading of poems, the thunderous speeches were endeavors of "men." He admired men who could stand up and improvise stirring flowery speeches at funerals and political gatherings. He valued such things.

With the Algerian poem, I entered into my grandfather's plans—as undefined, as far-fetched as all our plans were. There were plans for a house of stone, a house with pillars, on the grounds of my grandfather's vineyard, right alongside Beaufort Castle itself: the Crusaders' monument matched by the Ajami's monument. There were plans for quiet homes and lives for the young unmarried women. There were constant plans to shop around for a wife for my Uncle Ahmad and his constant evasions. There were plans for my father's return. And now, the reading of the poem on Algeria, the intimations of some talent for language, the weakness for books, had added one young boy to the family's plans. I had made my contribution to my mother's campaign. When my father returned, the small boy he left behind, the boy with black cotton frocks, would have going for him the sanction of the patriarch of Arnoun.

His own four sons had already made their choices. The oldest, my Uncle Hussein, had married earlier than my grandfather had wanted, in the village where he was assigned to teach. Burdened with children, my Uncle Hussein was trapped. He had his love affairs and his family and his impractical ways. My Uncle Ahmad, the second son, was single and he was "odd." My grandfather was

forever silent about Ahmad. My father, the third son, had not been cut out for the world of books and learning. The youngest, my Uncle Abbas, had gone further in schooling than his older brothers. But he, too, had made a different choice when he had made his way to Sierra Leone. Perhaps I could be a *mujtahid*, a mullah, my grandfather thought. But clerics were shabby then, and they were obscurantists. They were of a world I was allergic to. They were of the old world. It was the glitter of the world beyond ours, the modern enclave of Beirut—the Armenian girls, the films, the soft ice cream I bought downtown, the tumult of new politics—that held me. The bearded mullahs were of a world we were just beginning to shed. Even my grandfather floated the idea and then abandoned it in favor of the idea of modern schooling. The old man had not forgotten his own passage, so long ago, to the shrine cities of Iraq and the religious seminaries, his own dread of the privation he had seen.

It wasn't just the distant fight in Algeria that was new. A vendor at a falafel stall close to my school hung a photo of a smiling man with a large nose, the Egyptian Gamal Abdel Nasser. The obscure officer had suddenly jumped to stardom: Nasser going to a conference of Afro-Asian leaders in Bandung, Nasser telling the Americans to go drink the water of the Mediterranean, Nasser alone beating the French and the British and the Israelis in the Suez War in 1956. The Egyptian suddenly cast a long shadow over our country. They loved him in the Basta quarter, the Sunni stronghold. They saw him as the standard-bearer of Arab nationalism, perhaps as a link to an older time when the truth of Sunni, urban Islam held sway. They were "orphans of the Sultans," it was said of the Sunnis. The passing of the Ottoman Empire, the demise of Muslim rule, the very creation of this small Lebanese republic had unsettled them. In the Egyptian, they saw a counter

to the pull of the country westward. It took little time for Nasser to hit his stride. Before him, speeches had been in sonorous, cumbersome, and stilted classical Arabic. He took to the radio with great ease. He found his themes: he mocked the Great Powers and their local cronies—agents, he called them. The speeches became accessible, even incendiary, in their language, the language of daily life. It was hypnotic, the voice of Nasser on the radio as you walked the streets of West Beirut.

It was said of the Egyptian that he was an upstart, that he was the son of a postman. The radio stations in Arab capitals opposed to Nasser played a song about lovers burdening postmen with so many letters. It was a way of putting down the Egyptian, reminding all of his humble origins. But those who conceived a romance for him believed that he would turn upside down the order of things.

The new politics came to my elementary school in the relentless obsessions of a Palestinian teacher by the name of Mohamed al Assad and a teacher from the town of Bint Jbeil in South Lebanon by the name of Ali Bezzi. Mohamed al Assad, a large, curly-haired young man with an abundance of energy, had a frenzied passion for all things political. Teacher Ibrahim wanted the young man from Haifa to remember that he was working without a permit from the exalted Ministry of Education; he wanted him to stick to the material he was supposed to teach, to prepare the students for government examinations, to administer the punishments.

On a November day, probably in 1956, Mohamed al Assad set aside our school work and railed against something called the "Balfour Declaration" or the "Balfour Promise." Balfour, a British scoundrel, had promised Palestine to the Jews, Mohamed al Assad said. Our teacher didn't supply the details of the Balfour

Declaration or its meaning or the year it had been issued; he only said that this was the anniversary of the Balfour Promise, and we should all go on strike to let the world know what we thought of Balfour and his promise. We didn't know whether Balfour was dead or alive, but we were happy to go out and march down the neighboring alleyways denouncing his name. It was an opportunity to cut classes, and it was welcomed.

But the episode didn't sit well with Teacher Ibrahim. He warned that the parents were spending what they earned by "the sweat of their brow" to send their children to school. There was nothing to be gained from strikes and demonstrations. The Ministry of Education could crack the whip, shut down the school, bring ruin to Teacher Ibrahim and everyone associated with the school. The Palestinian schoolteacher was working off the books, Ustadh Ibrahim warned. A government inspection could put him out on the street. Mohamed al Assad understood all that Teacher Ibrahim said, promised obedience, and then went about mixing politics with schoolwork. He smuggled the politics into Arabic composition, into the grammar, into the hopeless history course. "OK, boys, conjugate for me, 'The Arab people shall return to Palestine.'"

"Tell me again, boys, who are the traitors who sold Palestine?"

"The Hashemites of Jordan and King Farouk of Egypt."

"What is our most malicious enemy?"

"Imperialism!"

"Well done, boys, the sons of the Arab world will set the world right in due time."

Ali Bezzi peddled his own politics. He said he was a Baathist. Two young Syrians in Damascus, one a Sunni Muslim, the other a Greek Orthodox, had spun out the theory of the Baath, of "resurrection," while they were studying in Paris. The Arabs, said the

Baathists, were one people. But the Arabs were in slumber and needed resurrection. The old social classes would be overthrown; the fake boundaries separating the Arab countries would be dismantled. "Arabism is love," said one of the two founders. The Baath ideology had caught on in Ali Bezzi's hometown of Bint Jbail, on the Lebanese-Israeli border. No one had an explanation why the town of Bint Jbail had given such a great reception to the Baathist view. Sons of peasants had taken up the ideology, had sat around in Bint Jbail's square and repeated the pronouncements of the Baath.

Ali Bezzi didn't explain much about the Baath. His Baathism was part of his own view of himself as someone marked and someone special. He did say that the Baath stood for "unity, liberation, and vengeance." The "trinity" was attractive and emphatic: first there would be Arab unity, then liberation, then vengeance against Israel and the West. Vengeance stayed with me. Vengeance was what men resorted to when women dishonored them, when strangers killed their cousins or their brothers, when they were deprived of a piece of land that they believed to be theirs. Ali Bezzi's ideology left me cold, though. There was something at once cruel and pedantic about him. He took a little too much pleasure in disciplining the students who ran afoul of his rule. We disliked him and, thus, we disliked his politics.

Ali Bezzi's trinity did not fool Teacher Ibrahim either. The older custodian of the school suspected the young ideologue. He saw a scoundrel; he saw through the mask—or at least that was what he said when Ali Bezzi finally played his hand. The young ideologue was busy courting the students of the National School and their parents. After building a reputation for himself, he opened his own school in a nearby alleyway. Teacher Ali Bezzi became Principal Ali Bezzi. The Baath politics were forgotten.

Ali Bezzi now had the coveted school license that the Ministry of Education could suspend—he had things to lose. This man would not be tilting at windmills.

The new politics didn't always betray; nor were they always pedantic and sullen. At least they weren't when they came to our doorstep, where we lived, brought there by Salah, a charming, young Communist, then twenty years of age, when I was about twelve.

Salah came for one of the neighbor's daughters. But it often seemed that he was there for the political discussion. Engrossed in the discussion, he forgot about the tall, handsome young woman he was courting. Salah was chatty, with a temperament both idealistic and gentle. He loved his words. But the words never imprisoned him. With all of us huddled around a few smoldering pieces of coal, over strong glasses of tea prepared by Umm Abdu's husband, the "wretched Damascene," Salah put forth his politics. The politics were a mix of the outrageously irreverent, the daring, the comic. Most of the time it seemed that Salah's new politics were an intentional affront to his father, Abu Salah.

An eight-hour working day was Salah's first demand. This was put before men and women who took toil as a given, who accepted that men and women worked from the cradle to the grave, as they put it. Salah had other ideas as well—loftier and more subversive. The land of convents and monasteries and Muslim religious endowments had to be distributed to the farmers. Electricity had to be provided at reduced prices. Foreign firms had to be nationalized. Medical care was a right, said Salah. It was from Salah that I heard the grand declaration: "From each according to his abilities, to each according to his needs."

It was from Salah, too, that I heard the first attack on one of the sacred incantations of the place, the expression of the ages:

Inshallah, Allah willing. *Inshallah* conditioned every plan, every promise, every appointment made. *Inshallah*, the bureaucrat sending the burdened supplicant on so many errands will have the forms all signed and ready. *Inshallah*, if Allah willed, there will be crayons for the schoolboys, a new pair of shoes for the *Eid al Fitr*.

Salah declared the expression *Inshallah* and those who used it "relics" who belonged in the "museum of history."

Salah read the pamphlets, attended the cell meetings. But Abu Salah knew his country. Tipped off by the ancestors, Abu Salah declared the new politics gibberish. There were *beys*, lords, and there were commoners. *Beys* commanded and ordinary men obeyed. Everyone knew that there were six Shia families who were entitled to seats in Parliament, to Cabinet posts. Need Abu Salah remind everyone of the names of the six families?

The seats in the country's Parliament—the seats that gave a handful of men the coveted and special license plates for their cars, the seats in Parliament that turned women's heads—were fixed and were always divisible by eleven: six Christians for every five Muslims. There could have been fifty-five seats, or sixty-six, or ninety-nine. The *beys* controlled the seats in Parliament. A few men, new men with new money, gave money to be elected on their Parliamentary slates. Those *beys* were part of the truth of each community in this checkered country.

Abu Salah swore by the name of one old *bey*, Ahmad bey al Assad, head of the leading family in the south of Lebanon. A picture of Ahmad Bey, with his red fez and with his famous mustache, adorned Abu Salah's home. And once, Abu Salah had been lucky enough to have met and shaken hands with the *bey*. Ahmad Bey was "our *bey*." Abu Salah savored the triumphs of the old *bey*. His face lit up when he speculated as to how many

women had found their way to Ahmad Bey's palace in the town of Tayyiba. There were stories of Ahmad Bey's strength, Ahmad Bey's honor. Salah's father had planned to one day present Salah to the *bey*. But now that Salah had lost his bearings, Abu Salah had abandoned the project.

Abu Salah knew his country. A few years earlier, he reminded everyone, some youngsters had flocked under the banner of a fiery orator, a troublemaker, who had returned to Lebanon from South America. Abu Salah had prophesied a bad end for the newcomer. Antun Saadah was his name. The son of Lebanese immigrants to Brazil, Saadah had returned to the old country with a vision he had glimpsed of a bigger world. To the land of clans and feuding religious sects, Saadah brought a new gospel—the kind of fantasies that had seized hold of Germany and Italy in the 1930s.

An intense personality cult surrounded Antun Saadah. Young men followed him even though they didn't know who his father was. A shrewd man, Antun Saadah must have been. He must have figured out that even men dissatisfied with hierarchies and *beys* and lords ached for new ways of submission. He came preaching "new politics." He gave them a swastika-like badge as an icon of their own. He talked about the unity of Greater Syria, exalted the race of the "Syrian Nation" in the same way the Nazis exalted the German race. He said that the "Syrian Nation" had nothing to do with the darker Egyptians. He loved militias and military salutes and uniforms and put together a paramilitary force of his own. He offered himself as a new leader, a messiah. He saw further than the old rulers with their red fezzes and their pot bellies. But Abu Salah, made weary and wise by a world he knew so well, was not impressed. Abu Salah reminded his son, and the younger schoolboy sharing his son's winks and taunts of his father, that he had known the thing would end. Abu Salah

knew that the six Shia families and the twenty-one other families that divided the country would not tolerate Saadah for long. Sure enough, in 1949, two years after he had returned from South America, when the schoolboy was still in his mother's lap, and Salah was still a boy with a runny nose, Saadah was put to death. It was Riad al Solh—the prime minister with the red fez and as many *dunams* of land as the eye could take in after whom my older brother had been named—who had ordered the execution of the South American adventurer. "Sons of whores, idiots—those followers of Saadah did not learn the lesson of Saadah's death. They go on talking about the *zaim*, the leader, as though he was going to return from the dead and make this land the land of milk and honey."

What were the new politics to Abu Salah! Abu Salah knew the sayings and the parables. He knew more sayings than anyone in the alleyway:

— Oppression hides in every heart: power reveals it, weakness conceals it.
— Envy lurks in every heart.
— Some men eat the goose, and some go to bed hungry.
— You have a piaster, you are worth a piaster.
— The white piaster for the black day.
— God gives sovereignty to whomever He chooses and withholds it from whomever He chooses.
— He who marries my mother, I will call him my stepfather.
— *Al Dahr Ghaddar*, fate is vengeful.
— Preserve what is old; what is new will not last.
— Older than you by a day, wiser than you by a year.

— If you were told that a mountain moved, believe it; but if you were told that a man changed his nature, don't believe it.

— If the owl is good enough to eat, the hunter wouldn't have ignored it.

— The low ground gets its share of water and the share of others.

Abu Salah knew the parched earth of South Lebanon and its merciless sun. He knew that the Litani River made its way to the sea past thirsty villages, past women struggling to the wells with jars on their heads. Abu Salah knew that after the dead were buried, the living fought over the rocky pieces of land they left behind. He knew that gullible men were devoured by the world. Were God to give *mulk*, sovereignty, to new men, Abu Salah knew what they would do with the *mulk* without bothering to listen to their promises and to their new words. He knew that they, too, would strut and that Abu Salah would have to fawn when he came into their presence. He would have to bow in front of men the names of whose fathers he didn't know.

The world came as it did. Its ways were known. And he, Abu Salah, knew these ways. And why should he delude himself? The country was stubborn, the landscape hemmed in, and the memories of men long and unforgiving. Abu Salah owed it to his son to stiffen his spine. He owed the same to the giggling schoolboy. The giggling schoolboy's father was away. When he returned, he, like Abu Salah, would not be taken in by the nonsense peddled by Salah and shared by the schoolboy.

A few years before Salah's and my time, the spirits inhabited the world of men. The spirits turned up: they came from the *wa'ar* to Arnoun. They showed up at the well, right by my mother's side,

when she wasn't looking. And the spirits promised my mother that there was an end in sight to this backbreaking toil, to the degradation. The spirits promised that doors would be opened for my mother's youngest child. The spirits told my mother that the eldest born to my father's second wife was going to be a girl—a revenge, a partial triumph, for my mother. And the next year, during a particularly difficult time in Arnoun, the spirits assured the brokenhearted daughter of the Abdullahs that a child would be born to Ali Ajami and his new wife who would be "unlike other children," a child whose disease would bewilder physicians in places near and far. The spirits delivered.

One spirit, a friendly one, showed up to remind my grandmother of religious duties to the dead that she had neglected. The spirits promised to carry out deeds of revenge, promised that husbands would remain enthralled with their wives, promised hidden treasure and peace of mind and good health. The spirits showed up as peasants were plowing the stubborn earth of Arnoun. Rashid Mousa dropped the sickle from his hand when a spirit whose acquaintance he had made confirmed to him his worries about what a scheming relative had in mind for him. The spirits explained why a man was feeling ill or was persistently unlucky. In the stark earth, under a sun that was so low it could be touched by a twenty-foot *ghul*, man-monster, the spirits provided some mist and some foliage.

There came a time—Salah's and mine—when the spirits were expelled. No one was sure that the spirits were fully exorcised. But the fellowship with the spirits had come to an end. Hitherto the spirits had existed right alongside the rocks and the IOU notes and the handmill with two stones. When my mother explained that a jar was broken because there was an evil spirit in it, the explanation reined in the fury of my grandmother who

had to replace the jar with a new one bought from the town of Nabatiyya. And the woman who refrained from sweeping the grounds of her hovel or of her father-in-law's house at night for fear that the spirits might be disturbed. Was that her way of saying that she had done enough work for a day, that it was now time to give her weary bones some badly needed rest?

It was a time between seasons. Men had not yet learned safer, more banal ways of explaining defeat and misfortune. With the spirits being told to pack up and leave, men were left facing one another. The new pamphlets—translated pamphlets from Russia, pamphlets spun out by the brave among us—promised to stand between man and the other man, promised to still greed, to rein in passions. New incantations were alternately merging with old ones.

Political passions—Salah's and the more furious ones to come—were burdened with men's hopes. Everyone must have known that the ways of our world—the ways of mothers and step-mothers, the ways siblings fought over contested pieces of land—would not give. It was futile to hope that miserly Hafiza, the cruel new wife of Teacher Ibrahim, could be taught new ways. It was futile to believe that fathers would refrain from slapping their sons across the face or belittling them in public. There was no hope that my mother would forget the details of her life in my father's village. And it was sure, as sure as anything, that Salah's father was bound to dwell on the valor and cleverness of one young man of Salah's age who had gone off to Africa and accumulated a fortune. The size of the fortune amassed in Africa varied with the mood of Salah's father. The more he wanted to belittle Salah, the larger the fortune of that other young man, whom Salah grew to hate without ever meeting.

Rearranging the vast world of politics, remaking history, dividing it into "epochs" and "stages" and neatly breaking down a whole society into categories and classes: that was the antidote to immutable ways. It was known that men wanted chaste virgins for wives—and always would. It was known that fathers terrified their sons and daughters—and always would. It was known that some men got away with it all, ate the goose, as they said, that others lost out—and always would. It was known—it was "written," it was foretold—that the man over there would spend a lifetime wishing ill for others, hoarding what came his way.

A "realistic" man pondering the ways of his people here had two choices: he could break down and cry. Or he could get himself some great doctrine that induced in him hope—and put him in a trance.

In every way it could, the country said that nothing beyond the familiar, beyond its arrangement of things was possible. The clerics of the rival sects in the country prohibited any original thoughts, anything beyond the strictures of what they sanctioned. The prime minister with the carnation in his lapel and his ever-present cigar, racing through the streets of the city in his official car with a coveted license plate—License Plate Number 3—asked men not to dream. He asked it of them in the finicky way he took in the crowds and the streets through the window of his car. The great merchant families who had the foreign concessions and the agencies rendered the same advice. So did the editors of the city's papers who had on file the same pictures of the same men and women and who ran the same pictures day after day.

The women loaded with expensive gold bracelets—from the wrist to the elbow, was the way it was described—asked of losers, of men without means and without power, not to dream. The

inviting glances were reserved for men with pieces of land to their name, for men graced by success, for "real men" who outwitted and triumphed over other men. It was in the presence of these "real men" that women purred and flirted. In the presence of the losers, the women only scowled. Losers had a way of bringing out virtue in women. They could not dream.

Yet just on the other side of this sobering view lurked its opposite: everything is possible, the familiar and the known on one side of the tightrope and the fantastic on the other. The right incantations and the right charms and the right throw of the dice would conceivably remake the world. My mother's petitions to the saintly imams could one day come through: my father would then be punished, and there would be bliss for my mother's two sons. Salah's incantations could bring about the millennium. Khalil could really find that one large diamond and that one gullible African who would give it to him. Doors would then be opened in front of Khalil—the doors of government ministers and officials, the doors of pretty women. As in the folk tales, the beggar could become a king and the king a beggar.

Before he acquired his wonderful lamp, Alaeddin was a wasted youth, the son of a pauper. Then fate came calling. Badr al Baddur, the beautiful daughter of the sultan, fell for the pauper's son: "And Alaeddin lived with his wife in all pleasure and fullness of life and escaped every danger. Then when the Sultan died, Alaeddin, his son-in-law, was seated on the throne of the Kingdom. He commanded and administered justice and all the people loved him. He lived with his wife in total happiness until there came to him the destroyer of delights…."

Ma'aruf, the poor cobbler of Cairo, was henpecked, married to a shrew who made his life a burden and a torment. From Cairo's torment a friendly *jinee* took that miserable son of Adam

to the Kingdom of Ikhtiyan-al-Khatan. There, all his wishes were fulfilled: the Sultan's daughter succumbed to him; he was given a magic ring that summoned a *jinee*. The *jinee* was lord over seventy-two tribes of *jinn*, each tribe was two-and-seventy thousand strong. Each *jinee* commanded a thousand giants, each giant a thousand goblins, each goblin a thousand demons, and each demon a thousand imps. All were tools of Ma'aruf the cobbler.

The cobbler became a king. King Ma'aruf reigned for many joyful years. He reigned until, like Alaeddin, he was visited by death, the destroyer of delights, the leveler of mighty kings and humble peasants.

In a world with hierarchies and verities cast in iron, the imagination soared. Reality demanded strict adherence. Men took it as it came and went about dreaming of the magic lamp. They fed off dreams—and obsessions.

But like some great avenger, the dream leveled things in its way. Men and women were vanquished—you could see them under the weight of custom and of terror; you could see them battling immense odds. It was hard to see what prevailing would mean, hard to believe that there would be much left in these weary souls to savor the triumph when it finally came. And when the triumph did come, could one be sure that the victory stood on solid ground? The evil eye, the envy of others: could those not undo what had come the victor's way?

Beggars became kings. Paupers became men of fortune whose fame reached the far corners of the earth. From the eyes of others, they now drew the glances of approval and supplication they wanted. In the midst of misery, they reigned. They commanded—and men obeyed and women submitted.

But deep within the eyes of those submitting to them, the victors caught dark insinuations and threats and yearnings. That

man on his knees, too, would one day want to become king. Didn't men kiss hands and ask God to break the hands that they were kissing? The world giving approval and supplication itself before the winner: Was it not awaiting the winner's undoing?

The world gave. And then, just as easily, just as suddenly, it took away.

V

I must have "jinxed" the country in 1958, when the independent republic of Lebanon was fifteen years of age and I was thirteen, groping out of boyhood years into the clumsiness of adolescence. I had crossed a line to go to a Christian school with a church attached to it and with a charming, wily abbot as its supervisor.

I had moved out of my mother's world that year. My father had prevailed in Saudi Arabia. The gypsy who prophesied fortune for him was right. Two four-story apartment buildings were built where my father's school and his house by the swamp had stood. There was money to go beyond elementary schooling, to enroll at a school in a more polished part of town. There was money for a new home in a quiet residential street of West Beirut. Into that household came four of my six half-brothers and sisters on my father's side. And like so many things in my life, it was all sudden—it had no connection with the life that I had been leading.

I had known the oldest three of my half-siblings when I had lived in the house by the swamp, but I had lost track of them in

the intervening five or six years. Most likely they had been in boarding schools, for my step-mother had joined my father in Saudi Arabia a couple of years after he had gone there. But my father now wanted his children brought up together. We were bearers of two different kinds of tradition. My older brother and I had known the life of our extended clan. We had the burden of my mother's experience, the burden of her divorce. The younger children were the product of an entirely different experience. My father wanted to bridge the gap in the classical Muslim standoff between the sons and daughters of rejected former wives and the sons and daughters of favored wives.

Vast Muslim kingdoms and small clans bedeviled by this problem knew no peace. The sons of abandoned wives inevitably lost out. The nature of the family in the Muslim world—the primacy of "blood" as a way of defining the family, the capricious and brittle ways of fathers that had to be mediated by mothers—left the stepchildren in the margins. Intrigue governed the world of the family. Lives wasted away waiting for small plots of land, for what property was there to be divided among those waiting for the capricious to be summoned before the Almighty.... In this kind of game, it was hard for the stepchildren to emerge intact. My father could not stitch the fault line between his two sets of children.

Our new home was a large apartment in a building with an elevator—a quiet building that never adjusted to our coming and goings. A decade after we had left our ancestral village behind us, we were now clearly within the city. Its ways and security were not fully ours, but we were within the gates—new telephone number and all. Our neighbor across the hall was Awni, a celebrated dressmaker to whose door came the smart set.

It fell to my Aunt Sakiba, who presided over my father's household, to see us all into the world of the city. Sakiba was my unmarried aunt. Suitors had come for her in years past, but she had spurned them. She was an independent woman, the kind to unnerve suitors and their mothers. She was left with a vast domain of nephews and nieces, children of her brothers and sisters working in faraway places. Denied a small family of her own, she was left with the entire clan. She had ideas for everyone: dreams for her nephews, more protocol and self-improvement for her brothers and sisters. She took it upon herself to put a touch of modernity upon her father, the old Shaykh of Arnoun. She picked his shirts and the right pieces of cloth for his suits. The proud man indulged her and went along. There was always a special regard for her—the unmarried daughter with uncertain prospects. Besides, she carried his mother's name. He who treasured the memory of his mother passed this affection onto the unmarried daughter.

It was my Aunt Sakiba who knew of the "better schools" and who dispatched us there. There was a fancy American prep school in West Beirut, a number of French schools in Christian East Beirut and in Jounieh, a Christian Maronite suburb by the sea. Sakiba's countless nephews and nieces would swarm over these schools. She would take us there, always aware that she had to do us proud on these occasions. Sharply dressed, ready with the right sorts of questions, she delivered us into the custody of the principals of those schools with the assurance that the tuition would be paid on time, that they would have in her a reliable partner, that our family treasured learning and the world of learning, that our parents in faraway lands were toiling to give us a world better than the one they themselves had known.

My mother had her phobias about the company of "strangers," especially about the *Nasranis*, the Christians—about their

schools and their food and their ways. She may have said a word or two, probably in passing, probably with a sense of humor and resignation, about her two sons going to a school with a church and an abbot. But having recorded her objections, my mother was glad that we were on our way. She remained in the Armenian-Shia squatter settlement where we all had our start with two of her older children.

My older cousin Nadia was our secondary school's bright star. Her father was away in Africa. If he turned up at all, it was only for short visits, and I don't think he ever returned to stay. Nadia's mother was a sister of my paternal grandmother's. But the sisters partook of different cultures: Nadia's mother had no interest in religious rituals. She wore well-tailored suits and high-heel shoes, and she wore no head cover, not even a scarf. She had passed onto her daughter her independence. Nadia must have been the most emancipated young woman of her time. Not for her were the stern injunctions against looking men in the eye or against crossing her legs in the presence of strangers. There had been no father around to bully her. The spunky young woman, who lived in a "modern" part of the city, right on the edge of the Christian quarter of Achrafiyeh was light years ahead of her clan—through and through a city girl. She knew what she favored: the old world behind her was of no interest to her; it could not hold her or rein her in. Nadia could hold her own in any conversation. Nadia knew how to roll her "r" in that special way that the French "r" had to be rolled in Lebanon; Nadia knew how to speak French *comme il faut*. Nadia would tell glamorous tales about Paris, would speak of the fabled city she had never seen as though it had been her town. She mocked a relative who had gone to Paris and come back to describe his visit to the Eiffel Tower for having done something that only first-time visitors to Paris

did. She knew movies and movie stars and the ins and outs of their personal lives; she was a voracious reader of novels. (Some years later, life would imitate art when Nadia wrote to her favorite Egyptian novelist. He wrote back, and she went to live with him in Cairo for a while.)

I was younger than Nadia—and star-struck. She was good to me and allowed me to move in the outer orbit of her gang. A number of us Muslims at school had been given the dispensation to be on our own when the rest of the school attended the service at church. Nadia's banter and self-confidence in this setting was remarkable. A couple of times, she slipped into the back row of the church and came back full of wonder, full of praise, perhaps of envy, for the grace of the ceremony.

It was a blessed time. My father was away; I was a step removed from my mother's grief and sorrow. Schooling was a much gentler affair. The cruelty of the school that had been put up by my father, a school with no roots and no love of learning, was behind me. Our abbot, whose name I never knew (I only knew he was Abuna al Shammas, Our Father, the Abbot), was a gentle soul who loved conversation and banter. He paid us, the few Muslim students, special attention, made sure we felt at home.

Around us, in the city, it was still perhaps a time of innocence. The story of that year, I remember, the story everyone loved, the story that inspired skits and clever lines, was the scandal about a prostitution ring led by a "madam" with the working name of Afaf, Chastity. Afaf's accomplice was a government prosecutor by the name of Shukri Saba. He had given Afaf cover and protection, and she had run a prostitution ring which catered to men of means. Her working girls had been "respectable" young women who had gone to school—some even were housewives, perhaps. Our city had a large brothel in the center of town—*suq*

al sharameet, the market of prostitutes, it was called—that was the low end of the market, for working men, for villagers on an excursion to the city. But Afaf and the prosecutor had still managed to shock the city.

From this bliss, we were awakened by the eruption of a civil war that would play itself out that summer. It happened quickly. I remember scurrying to get home from the predominantly Muslim part of the city where our school was located on the first day of fighting—the sound of bullets, the panic all around, the sudden appearance everywhere around us of barricades with armed men, sandbags behind which young men with rifles and machine guns proclaimed their defiance of the government. Nasib Metni, the publisher of *The Telegraph* (the newspaper that had once published a letter to the editor from my father about the dreadful condition of the southern countryside) and a figure in the opposition to the government, was struck down by a hail of bullets at midnight as he was walking the short distance from his office to his home after putting the final touches on that morning's paper. A man of the left, he had been a thorn in the side of the country's president. His murder was to serve as the spark for a political conflict that had been gathering force for some time. We were sent home by the abbot, who had to worry about his school, about making it home in his distinctive garb past Muslim street gangs. The USIS Library close to my home—the library of the United States Information Service—was sacked. The books with plastic covers and borrowers' cards and titles on the spines were taken out and scattered over the pavement. No tears were shed for the books of the Americans: books about nature and geography, quaint volumes about American pioneers. The books were denounced as works of imperialist propaganda. A loudspeaker

on top of a van called the *shabab*, the young men, to rebellion. A cable car was put to the torch.

It was not quite a Christian-Muslim war that had erupted, though there was a measure of that. Boulos Meouchi, the Patriarch of the Maronites, had sided with rebels against the Christian president; for his sins, he was to earn the name of Muhammad Meouchi from the hardliners among his people who felt that he had deserted them in battle. A larger clash between radical Arab nationalism, led by the Egyptian Gamal Abdul Nasser, and the Americans was to be fought out in Lebanon. The country of religious sects, the country of clans had become a battleground between East and West—it was a fight that glamored our small republic.

The younger people in my clan were swept up in the politics of Arab nationalism, in the passions called forth by Nasser. Not so far from the apartment building where we lived, Saeb Salam, the former prime minister and the self-designated leader of the opposition known for his trademark fresh carnation in his lapel, had his headquarters in a house that had been the seat of his father's power.

We knew the villain of the affair was the pro-American President Camille Chamoun. Chamoun was a crafty politician, but he was carried away by overweening ambition. The small country had always been parceled out among the big men: Chamoun sought to monopolize it. He had once presented himself as a Lebanese champion of the Palestinian cause. The ambitious Christian politician had spoken of its loss as a tragedy that recalled the loss of Granada; he now presented himself as America's hope in the region. He was shrewd, Camille Chamoun. He befriended John Foster Dulles, spoke the great Cold Warrior's language; he had been solicitous of Dwight Eisenhower when

the American leader had suffered a heart attack. Chamoun had been banned by the country's constitution from running for a second term. But the handsome man with steel gray hair was not one to be easily discouraged. He reminded followers and adversaries alike that his middle name was Nimr, Tiger. Camille "Tiger" Chamoun would run roughshod over the unwritten rules of the place. He packed the Parliament—the body entrusted with electing a president—with his own men, saw to it that the leaders of other communities, the other big men, were defeated in a rigged round of elections. And he presented his campaign to the Americans as their cause. The Beiruti politician who loved his hunting hounds and safari suits and dark sunglasses said that he was America's man, bragged that he had the Americans in his back pocket.

No one was sure about the Americans. Rumors circulated that the American ambassador, Robert McClintock—nicknamed "Rapid" McClintock—disliked Chamoun and was determined to push him out of office. The movements of Rapid McClintock were closely followed. The comings and goings of his black Cadillac—identified by an American tag, led by a machine-gun-mounted jeep, accompanied by a motorcycle escort—were scrutinized for some verdict on the Americans. It was said that McClintock had reached an understanding with Kamal Junblatt, the Druze chieftain in the Chouf Mountains above Beirut. There was a deep animus, a vendetta between the Druze chieftain and the Maronite president. They may have been allies some years back, when they were both men of the Chouf Mountains and before great battles had been fought between Maronite and Druze. Now it was known that McClintock thought highly of the Maronite Patriarch, another adversary of Chamoun.

We fled for a house in the hills, in a small town in the Chouf Mountains. We would wait out Beirut's troubles and the humid summer, we thought, in that hill town. An aunt of mine, a sister of my father's, lived there with her husband and children. Her husband, an officer in the gendarmes, a decent and humble man, was genuinely beloved in that Druze town. He knew the pride of the Druze, and he never ran afoul of it. He himself was from an influential clan in the Bekaa Valley. He knew the code of mountain people.

We rented a house close to his, a pretty house of white stone and a red-tiled roof in the middle of a vineyard. My older brother took up the accordion after a young man in our summer village put up his red and white accordion for sale.

But the civil war had spread; the Druze chieftain and the Maronite president were playing for big stakes. The fighting trailed us to our summer village. We packed everyone in my father's car and set out to our ancestral village in the south, away from Beirut and the hill towns around Beirut. My brother was full of distress when his red and white accordion was left in the heap of discarded things by the side of the road, unable to fit in the overstuffed car.

The US Marines landed on Beirut's shores in late July. Chamoun's great threat that the Americans were sure to come to the rescue had materialized. It was one of those crazy American errands into distant places. It had a wonderful name, that American expedition: Serenade at Dawn. They came because, on July 14, Iraq's pro-Western boy-king, King Faisal (a cousin of King Hussein of Jordan), was overthrown in a bloody coup. King Faisal was a harmless young man with a gentle face and soft eyes and small stature. Older men around him ruled with a heavy hand, while he, riding a ferocious tiger, tried to govern

a country known for its wild ways. The boy-king had a hated regent, his uncle, and, more importantly, he had a notorious prime minister, one Nuri al Said, a crafty politician then a year or two short of seventy. Nuri al Said had behind him a lifetime of intrigue. A former ally of the British, he distrusted the crowd and "the street" and the new radical politics. The crowd had reciprocated the sentiment. On that summer day in July of 1958, Nuri and the Hashemites had run out of luck. Two army brigades, with orders to go to Jordan, converged on Baghdad instead. The royal palace, Qasr al Rihab, had fallen to the rebels. The young king and his whole family, including his aging grandmother, were gunned down by the mutineers. Nuri himself eluded the crowd. A reward of two thousand dinars for Nuri dead or alive was offered, but no reward would be needed. Nuri was caught a day later in disguise as a woman covered with a black abaya. The mob that identified him killed him; his body was impaled and dragged through the streets.

Some dawn of a new age appeared in sight. The Arab world was about to sprout wings and fly away into the embrace of radicals and Communists and troublemakers. In our small republic by the Mediterranean, the Americans had decided to draw a line. Our country was the West's listening post and its bridge to the interior. It could not be allowed to slip away.

"Heat, Mosquitos Trouble Marines," reported *The New York Times* from Beirut on July 20th. "At night the mosquitos make life miserable. They are voracious and gather in enormous swarms to feast on the Americans. The mosquito repellent supplied to all Marines seems to do very little good."

The passion of the civil war was not my family's. We were still a people with private horizons and concerns. Nonetheless, the civil war—or at least its parody—found its way to our village.

The olive-colored cans of the American military—the canned food of a more glamorous world—was appearing in the city and even making its way into the villages of the country. I fell for the novelty of the whole thing, for the ease and convenience of the canned food compared to that of the elaborate meals prepared by my mother and aunts.

Guns and ammunition were coming in for the opponents of Camille Chamoun from Syria under the direction of the Egyptian Gamal Abdel Nasser, then president of the short-lived United Arab Republic that brought together the unwieldy Syrians and the orderly, graceful Egyptian into a doomed political union. A band of young villagers took off to Syria to bring back guns from Damascus. They left, escorted by a guide, under the cover of night and returned with rifles after two or three days of military training. One young man from the village, Abbas, son of a dear friend of my mother's from those unhappy years in Arnoun, was given the honor of bringing back a machine gun. Abbas was a *fatwa*, a real man—well-spoken, good at banter with women, commanding in the presence of other men. It was natural that Abbas would return with the machine gun. *Al shabab*, the young men, were welcomed home when they returned. They arrived to the ululation of women. Arms were the adornment of men, our culture thought. And the *Shabab* of Arnoun loved the new Czech rifles. They strutted around with them, carried them on their peasant errands to the threshing fields and the tobacco sheds. The remote countryside, stripped of its muskets so long ago by the forces of Ahmad Pasha, the Butcher, the master of Acre and Sidon, now gloried in the adornment of the rifles, the gifts of an Egyptian.

But the rifles—and the sole machine gun—were stored away to be sold when the civil war came to an end. The fight between those who wanted Lebanon to look across the Mediterranean to

the Western world and those who drew their inspiration from the Arab and Muslim East was being decided by men mightier than the villagers of Arnoun. Muslim West Beirut and the fierce Druze mountaineers were pitted against the American-backed regime. The Shia villages were then places of marginality and acquiescence.

In Arnoun, in the summer of 1958, less was said about the distant war in the city and in Mount Lebanon than about an affair between one of my great-uncles, one of the Alawiyya men, and Sakna, a young peasant woman.

My Great-Uncle Hassan Bey was a prosperous man, a land-owner in his sixties, with the fair skin of his family, with articulate sons and daughters Sakna's age and older. Sakna was a vital, dark *fellaha*, peasant woman, who had known the life that Arnoun had offered—the work of the land, the tobacco crop. She must have been sixteen or seventeen that summer. She was a large young woman with a full figure that her peasant dress clung to and flattered, marking out her ample breasts, her sturdy legs. She had the kind of beauty our peasant women had—the kind that was destined to fade quickly due to toil and poverty and repeated pregnancies. And she had that self-confidence (destined to be short-lived too) that came to a young woman possessed of a sudden appreciation of her womanly spell and powers.

My great-uncle had been a high official in the gendarmes. A few years back he had been cashiered from his position when he was caught taking tobacco in his official jeep to sell on the black market. The incident had left its mark on him and was always remembered. It wasn't that he had done something wrong. Everyone knew that a big man from the Bekaa Valley, a politician of standing and power, was one of the country's hashish growers and smugglers. (The hashish grower's son was a classmate of mine

at my prep school in the city, the only other Shia student there at the time.) The smuggling was part of the old man's mystique. The country was without qualms about such matters. Hashish growing glamored the politician from the rugged valley in the eastern part of the country. Men did such things. Hassan Bey, using his official jeep to elude the inspectors of the *Régie*, had been a failed smuggler: that was the burden in the shadow of which the old officer was to spend his years of retirement.

The substance of authority had been denied Hassan Bey. He was left with the memory of his previous power—and with some of its trappings: a swagger-stick that he carried under his arm, a safari hat that he wore on his walks in the village and whenever he went out to inspect the tobacco fields. He was fond of the old Ottoman title of Bey, sure to respond to those who used it to address him. But his was an unsure claim to his title. There had been the banishment from office, the forced retirement. Besides, by the late 1950s such titles were becoming a thing of the past. They were now reserved for the very few men who owned chunks of land and sat in the country's parliament, men who were given cabinet posts. My great uncles were losing claim to that grand title.

The clever peasants who worked the land had their way of getting around such aristocratic claims. A Najib Bey would be addressed by his oldest—and in his case, only—son's name and would become Abu Munir, father of Munir. The same went for Hassan Bey. Twenty years earlier that kind of familiarity would have been unthinkable. But a world—its authority and its familiar landmarks—was slipping away.

When the great power his rank in the gendarmes had given him was taken away, Hassan Bey was left with his tobacco crop. It was now his world and his dominion. He gave it his attention and his devotion. It was not that he needed its income to maintain

the life of the gentry. Hassan Bey still had a decent pension. The state had been kind enough to let well enough alone after it had cashiered him from his position.

It was the tobacco work that brought Hassan Bey and Sakna together. Prior to this summer, Sakna no doubt struck him as just another peasant of Arnoun, bearing the mark and the dark pigmentation of peasant work. He must have seen her countless times, making her way down from the spring by Beaufort Castle, swaying to balance the full jar of water on her head. Walking by the mausoleum where his parents were buried, he must have seen her, along with other village women, doing the wash, or cleaning heavy pots and pans in the village pond. It is doubtful if he, Hassan Bey, the landholder, the former officer of the gendarmes who in his youth had gone as far away as Istanbul, ever gave her a second glance.

This summer was a different story. Hassan Bey fell for the young *fellaha*. There were old ways, ways as old as the hills, for handling affairs between landholders and young, comely *fellaha*. But the old stocky man lost his bearing. He was smitten by the young *fellaha*. He threw caution to the wind, forgot the old ways.

Had Hassan Bey observed those old ways, he would have seen to it (with some discreet money of his own) that Sakna married a young man, a peasant boy, from her surroundings. After the marriage, Sakna's door would have been open to him. Who knows: a child might have been born to the young peasant couple who had the fair skin of the Alawiyyas. There would have been the usual malicious gossip. The place would have chewed on the matter, as it did so many other subjects, at dusk, on trips uphill to fetch water, on excursions to the Litani River to wash clothes. But no homes would have been wrecked. The gossips would have had their day with the story. But even they knew the ways of time: the hand of

fate was capricious. A peasant woman enjoying the tale of Sakna's dishonor had no assurance what her own young daughter, sweet and virtuous Mahsin, might do on a summer dawn when she set out with the other field hands to pick the tobacco leaves.

The young schoolboys spending their summers in the village went to the tobacco shacks, where the young peasant women did their delicate and fast work, in search of banter and excitement. This summer the visitors to the tobacco shack were joined by the old retired officer of the gendarmes. Hassan Bey no longer acted his age or his class. He stuck around the tobacco shack. Mischievous field hands told that he even helped Sakna with her work. He mingled with the field hands and became excessively friendly and understanding of their follies and their mishaps. Hassan Bey's sons and nephews had talked of a classless society where men would be equal, where each would contribute in accord with his abilities and would be provided in accord with his needs. The sons and the nephews were amateur Communists. They loved the irreverence that came with the word. They appreciated the distance that such a claim placed between themselves and their elders. The peasants of Arnoun had taunted the sophisticated boys and had asked whether they would be willing to do the work of the land when Communism came and the dunams of tobacco and the deeds to the land were taken away. It was typical Arnouni banter with the peasants at dusk. But there was Hassan Bey providing an example of his own of the gullibility of all of Bani Adam, sons of Adam.

It was told by a man good at telling such tales, masterful in the manner and timing of his narrative—casually breaking the narrative to roll his cigarette right when he knew that he had his audience's rapt attention—that some field hands had come upon Sakna and Hassan Bey fondling one another by a heap of

chaff near the threshing floor. When spotted, the two lovers had panicked, and Sakna began to conceal Hassan Bey under the chaff. "No use," she was told. "We can still see the bald red spot of his head."

It was recalled in the village of Arnoun how, some years back, the villagers had to go out and clear the harsh, unpaved road to Arnoun of stones whenever my Great-Uncle Najib Bey (the relative who had asked my mother to become his mistress before our move to Beirut) came to Arnoun to inspect his land and to make sure that the world had held in his absence. Najib Bey, the oldest of the Alawiyyas, was an official of the state and a colonel in the gendarmes. He lived in Achrafiyeh, a quiet Christian sub-urb in Beirut, in a large home that bore the mark of his military career; he was married to a woman of the city, a Sunni Beiruti woman who took pride in her family background, who looked on her husband's people as country yokels who were best kept at arm's length. He took the world as it came to him: there were landholders and sharecroppers, there were Beys and commoners, there were officials of the state and subjects of the state, there were dark-skinned men with *kafiyyas* like the peasants who worked his land and light-skinned men with blue eyes like himself, and like his brother, who owned the land. Najib Bey believed that the villagers were a treacherous lot. Underneath their obedience and their deference, he saw resentment and envy and rage. He believed that if they were given an ounce of freedom, they would begin to kill. The men on their knees, Najib Bey thought, had knives in their pockets and knives in their hearts. In his younger brother's summer of folly, the colonel saw a great menace to his world and to the prerogatives of his family.

At the beginning of this affair, when the thing seemed harmless, Hassan Bey's wife had shown her husband's fling little

concern. She had hoped that the old man would indulge himself and would then return to the "straight path." When her patience seemed to be feeding his foolhardy ways, the statuesque woman who came from a distinguished family and had some land of her own, who always carried herself with style and dignity, sat the old man down for a serious discussion. Hassan Bey was suddenly face to face with a final reckoning. He knew his wife: he knew that a drawn-out fight with her would be a searing battle into which she would throw all she had and in which she would be backed by her grown-up sons and daughters. Under the gun, Hassan Bey retreated. Young Sakna had to be sacrificed. As the summer drew to a close, it was learned that the young *fellaha* would be marrying into a neighboring village. For her, the dream of a house in Beirut and a life of plenty and ease was not to be.

The summer, too, sealed Chamoun's dream: the bid for a second presidential term was set aside. The Americans would not tie their prestige to his ambitions after all. Chamoun was succeeded by the commander of the army, a seemingly apolitical man, who had done his best to keep the army out of the civil war. It was said of the commander of the army, a quiet man with a French wife and no children, that he was a compromise choice arrived at by Egypt and the United States: two outside powers so prominent in the life of the country.

—⚍—

My great-uncle had his fling in the summer of 1958. The rest of us watched. My older brother and my cousins carved the date and their names on rocks at Beaufort Castle: pledges of friendship, a touch of immortality for times to come. On one rock were recorded the names of Riad and Qahtan, in honor of their

friendship in the summer of 1958. Another rock recorded the romance of one of my Alawiyya cousins—a generation older than the rest—and a young French woman who had returned with him that summer from France, where he was getting his medical education. The ways of men were fickle. And the rocks preserved those sentiments of a moment that once seemed like the sure fidelities of a lifetime.

No rock bore my signature. I spent a good deal of the summer in the company of my grandfather, in his shadow. Things rose and caved under. My grandfather remained himself. The feuds and the obsessions that seized others here were not for him. My great-uncles had quarreled with the peasants of Arnoun. They wanted more respect than was offered them. Everywhere they saw slights. Asserting dominion, they were challenged at every turn. Grave violations were read into the smallest of details.

My grandfather lived within the limits of his world. Between him and the people of Arnoun there was a bond that spared him rage and humiliation. There was no need for him to bully *ahl al balad*. What command, what presence he had in their lives came naturally to him. It was his due. He had more land than they did. Amidst an illiterate population, he could read and write, sign his own forms and government petitions. There had been his travels: his studies in Iraq, his passage to South America, his memories of the trips on horseback to the towns of Safad and Tiberias, to Huleh Lake, to Acre—towns and places now on the other side of an impenetrable divide. His sons and daughters had been spared the toil of the land. Moreover, it was clear that he was a healthy man who had marked time and who had survived harsh years and who now had the means to walk into the modern hospitals of the city if taken ill. He had made the pilgrimage to Mecca—both

a sacred religious obligation and a seeing of an adult life of means toward its proper fulfillment.

Yet for all these differences there was something of the peasantry of Arnoun in my grandfather. He had their dark color. He was in his element when he was among the Arnounis. And hard as my fastidious aunts would try to distance him from his world, to teach him proper manners and new pretensions, to remind him of the distance that had to be kept from the *fellaheen*, he remained rooted in his world. My grandfather was there, among the people of Arnoun, during weddings and funerals; he was there when "dreadful diseases" were announced, when a sudden pregnancy had to be seen to a quiet and proper resolution. "My dear young fellow, we all sow our wild oats and there is no need to tell you how many of these 'white beards,' men of seemingly solid honor, men feigning innocence, had done outrageous things in their time. Your generation did not invent sin. But in our time, we knew when things had gone far enough, and we knew when passions indulged had to be paid for."

Against the advice of my aunts, my grandfather invariably left his house at dusk and joined the peasants of Arnoun in the village square—in front of Arnoun's only shop, where Hassan Assaf, the shopkeeper, kept a few cans of sardines, some matches, a tin can of *halva*, and an ice box without ice with some lukewarm bottles of soda pop. Son of a wanderer from Persia, father of sons and daughters who took off to remote places, my grandfather was always a man at peace with his own world. There was a world of hearsay that he acknowledged: the schooling of his grandchildren, the desperate scramble of his sons and daughters for new money in faraway places. And there was the familiar world of custom and precedent that was his own.

I accompanied the old man as he made his way through his small world. I sat by his side as he took in the flights into fantasy of one wild Arnouni who related close brushes with hyenas, with snakes twenty feet long; as the tales of times past were recited and amended; as men entered into their verbal duels; as the cruelty of government officials and tobacco inspectors was lamented. I guided him back home with his flashlight through the still darkness of Arnoun—a stillness broken only by tinkling sheep bells. This was my grandfather's gift to me. There were things that young men had to learn if they were to remain within the fold, if they were to escape the scolding of other men, if they were not to be accused of betraying their *asl*, their origins and their roots. There were things that "boys raised by women" had to learn. It was my grandfather's mission to transmit these ways to me.

Loyalty, my grandfather taught, anchored the world. Men were the words they said to other men and the promises they kept. The revered imams my grandfather respected kept their words. The big men of times past who rode together on horseback to faraway towns made pledges they kept. That was the world my grandfather savored.

Fidelity and obedience to fathers was another maxim of my grandfather's world. The old man, no doubt, worried that my mother's ordeal at my father's hands and her tales of past misfortune could embitter me against my father beyond the possibility of reconciliation. In his quiet, stern way, my grandfather drew a line. Fathers were merciless, he taught: it was their way. But no rebellion against a father would be sanctioned in my grandfather's world. It could go nowhere, that rebellion. The threads would be hacked, but the support that every boy needed from a father would not be there when it truly mattered. No divorced woman could see a young man through, give him a place among men.

I needed what my grandfather taught; I needed his strength and drew on it. Unthreatened, he was never a frenzied or a cruel man. I knew that his small world could not sustain me. (After all there were so many claimants, circling one another, feuding with one another, to inherit the miserly acres of tobacco.) But I was grateful for his presence and his steady hand.

Tradition—if he, my grandfather, was its embodiment and representative—was being eroded. Rather like the collars of some of my grandfather's white shirts that he wore against the commands of my Aunt Sakiba, tradition was fraying at the edges. Proud and stubborn, tradition was refusing to acknowledge its obsolescence. Tradition leaned on so many things: memories of past splendor, the frenzy of hounded sons and daughters and the money these sons and daughters were accumulating in the shops of Freetown or the diamond fields "upcountry." Time, in one way threatening that tradition, bearing news of its imminent demise, was also on its side. Old age and frailties and death were coming to the rescue. To be sure, our tradition focused glaring lights on men. But there came a time when men looked away, traveled to places beyond censure and pain. "Know, O men, that the life of this world is but a thing to play at and a passing delight, and a beautiful show." Rain, our tradition taught, brought herbage to the world. Then things withered, turned yellow, and crumbled into dust. "The life of this world is nothing but an enjoyment of self-delusion."

My grandfather always seemed timeless, dateless to me. He was in his early eighties in that summer whose memory remains with me. His battles were behind him. My mother said that she knew him when he was a more capricious man. She referred to him as *al Jabbar*, the mighty, the capricious. This was not my impression of him. He neither pampered nor suffocated me. He

offered the support of the world he knew. He marked out its boundaries.

Around the corner there was a more furious version of tradition. The new version, embodied in my father, had the limits of the old tradition but none of its grace. The new version could pretend and flail about. But were you to scratch it, to take away its new pair of dark sunglasses and its neckties that were burdened with so much self-esteem, you were sure to find the old phobias.

VI

> Gentlemen of the jury, what is a father, a real father? What is the meaning of that great word? What is the immensely great idea behind that name?...Do you believe, gentlemen of the jury, that such questions can escape our children, let us say, in their teens and when they begin to reason? The sight of an unworthy father inevitably arouses painful questions in a boy's mind...He is given the conventional answer to this question. "He begot you and you are his flesh and blood and therefore you must love him."

The words are the public prosecutor's in Dostoevsky's *The Brothers Karamazov*. But that tale is a Russian tale: it is a tale of patricide. The father torments, and he is murdered.

The Muslim tale has been—and remains—different from its Russian equivalent. The patricide in the literature of late

nineteenth century Russia was a prelude to the Revolution of 1917. There is no peace between fathers and sons in Muslim life, but there is no such theme as patricide, no great historical break either. Here it was slow and continuous—a muzzled hell. The sun rises again over the same old impasse. Then the tale trails off. Patriarchy fails. Old age comes: dominion turns into dust. But sons do not, as a rule, break through to a world of their own.

Father, the "great word," was everything here. Sons carried the father's first name as their middle name; a man was *Ibn*, the son, of a particular father or he was lost. In this society a father tied himself to God; a father linked the blessing of God to his own blessing and acceptance of a child. Patricide was but one step short of killing God. And that was unthinkable. The father drew on our dominant clannish ethos of "blood" and lineage. Then, further tightening the noose, the father had going for him the unsentimental reality of property—land and buildings and deeds to land and buildings. And, finally, he did this triple bind one better. He always had at his disposal the power of easy divorce and all that went with it: the crushing defeat of his children's mother; the threat of new, and inevitably more favored, children; the addition of a hostile sorceress to the household in the person of a step-mother.

Tomcats, my mother said of fathers, devoured their kittens. Mothers protected their kittens. In our folklore, fathers were would-be cannibals. And in my own personal history, my mother's tales of my father seeped into me. They were in the deep recesses of my mind. They were there when my father reentered my life with his long American car, with his commanding manner.

The tomcat who had gone off to Saudi Arabia years earlier had been a relatively lean one. A photo of my father was left at school; another copy hung in my grandfather's house in Arnoun.

It was a photo of a man with a thin face—intense, drawn. It must have been taken while he was in his twenties. Now there was a man with a double-chin and an ample waistline. The intensity in the eyes—while not exactly inviting in the photo—was, in the real-life version before me, stern and forbidding. The face was red: as always for me, there between us was a pigmentation divide. It was as though we were of different races.

My father's second youngest child was five. He had the red hair and features of my father. He was a favored child. Wealth came to my father the year he was born. His face was that of prosperity, whereas the faces of the older children were those of misfortune. He had been born in a placenta, we were told. The "sack" had been preserved. Further good tidings were expected. The boy had his red hair long in a ponytail. A *nidr* had been made that his hair would only be cut on the grounds of the Shia shrine of Zaynab in Damascus: the shrine associated with my mother—a place of lament and virtue and defeat. My father's *nidr* had been a generous one. It must have been made during a particularly difficult or promising time, a tense time of anticipation. The *nidr* promised that the money, some of the *rizq*, the blessing and good fortune, given by God would be used to feed the poor on the grounds of the shrine. But that *nidr* had lingered. My father hadn't redeemed it as early as he should have. My father's mother had warned that the *nidr* should be redeemed as soon as possible. Otherwise, luck in business could dry up, a child could be taken ill, "open roads" could close up again.

We made the passage to the shrine in my father's new car. It was a journey that most of the faithful made on buses and in service taxis. My father came with the trappings of triumph to a place of sorrow. He surveyed the multitudes from a victor's angle

of vision. There he was a winner amidst shrunken and wailing men and women. We stood out, didn't fit in.

For me it was a passage of pain. I possessed those other memories and identifications with the shrine that came to me from my mother. The *nidr* had promised that the indigent on the grounds of the shrine would be fed. But there were so many there, and the *nidr* had called for more lamb than was slaughtered. In my memory of that pilgrimage, the episode ends in my father cursing the rabble who couldn't get enough and in the disappointment on the part of so many who were left out of pieces of the slaughtered lamb and who were not given a few coins in compensation. The generous *nidr* was redeemed with caution. Even a woman of Arnoun who happened to be there came close to losing out. But she, the poor woman, persevered and cut off my father's route of escape. Appealing to him, she told him that a broken heart on the grounds of the holy shrine, in the presence of virtuous Zaynab, would haunt its tormentors. He gave in and railed against the schemes and the ingratitude of the multitude.

My father had returned from Saudi Arabia with his wife, the mother of six of his children. But no victor—no woman-victor, to be sure—could withstand a sudden turn of fate. Soon, in a furious storm that pitted my father's wife against my grandfather and my resourceful aunts, the second wife left. My father divorced her (only to remarry her three years later). The divorce was a concession on my father's part to his sisters and his parents. My father was caught between his family's wishes and his own preferences. The former had won out. The man with sunglasses and a red face was never as independent, as mighty as he looked to me. Part of my father ached for his father's acceptance, for anointment as the favored son, for recognition for the race he had run, for what he had accumulated and put together. But my grandfather would

give no such seal of approval. My father was at the center of a large web. Loans on mortgaged pieces of land in the village had to be paid off. The escalating pretensions in the city were proving costly. Part of my father wanted to crow about his success in business. He loved the word *millionaire*; he loved to describe himself as a self-made man. But part of him wanted to hide, for he knew that cries of triumph brought petitioners in their wake, seekers of favor, relatives anxious to share in what the hunt had produced.

—✺—

From Kafka's *Letter to His Father*:

> From your armchair you ruled the world. Your opinion was correct, every other was mad, wild, meshugge, not normal. Your self-confidence indeed was so great that you had no need to be consistent at all and yet never ceased to be in the right. It did sometimes happen that you had no opinion whatsoever about a matter and as a result all opinions that were at all possible with respect to the matter were necessarily wrong, without exception. For me, you took on the quality that all tyrants have whose rights are based on their person and not on reason. At least so it seemed to me.

"My dear fellow," my father said to a politically active younger cousin of his, a Communist, "don't bother with these pamphlets. We wrote these tracts while you were still a child in your mother's lap. We know the landscape: we were there first. But there is no

bread in all this. The world of business and of affairs: that is the world of men." My father then recited the story of his passage to Saudi Arabia: the harshness of the land, the fierce competition he had encountered there, the running room his talent had made for him in the oil-bearing town of Dhahran and the vast oil fields around it. When in the mood he revisited the gun-running episode to Palestine, the arrival in the Armenian district some years later. In the small circle of our kinsmen, no journey had offered as much vindication as had my father's. He had known Communists and men of affairs. He, a self-made man, had conquered. The heat and the princes of Saudi Arabia had failed to subdue him. He was a mere "boy" when he smuggled guns to Palestine. And he was still so young when he took on the forbidding Kingdom of Saudi Arabia. No one ever gave him a break: he worked for it. It was an overwhelming story for impressionable sons and daughters to live up to. "Sons of so and so," he said of the Saudis, "they never give anyone a break. They are particularly allergic to anything Shia. You had to be a tiger to make it there with a first name like Ali. But, look, I knew them and I prevailed."

My father's history was like a sword unsheathed in the face of his sons. He was now a slumlord. He had buildings and rents to collect. "Manhood" and "toughness" were awarded like some badges of distinction to the son who returned with most rents, who intimidated the tenants of my father's buildings into paying what they owed. This was a task I loathed. The identity and the means given me by my father placed me at a distance from the tenants of his buildings. But it was only two or three years before that I had been on the other side. I recognized in the pleading petitioners, in the engaging conversationalists offering tea and discussing everything under the sun except the small matter for which I had come, in the mother of the beautiful girl, Hayat,

extending me an irresistible invitation to sit down and have tea with her and her daughter, fragments of my own life. Invariably, from those errands, I returned empty-handed.

In elaborating and embellishing his own history, my father was rewriting mine. Those early years of my childhood—years of hardship back in the village, of privation in the tin shack in the city—were struck out of the record. We had parachuted out of some void into this polished neighborhood, into this large home with a maid and telephone. In the humid and suffocating summer of Beirut, in the year that followed the civil war, my father rented for us a small cabin on one of the restricted beaches of Beirut. He would drop us there, at the Saint Simon Beach, in Beirut's southern outskirts, and give us a day by the sea. It was no small change in our lives, this cabin on the beach. He had earned it for us; it was his gift to us. At times he was filled with wonder over our new circumstances. He would contrast the luxury of the day at the beach, the meals we had bought with coupons, with the tyranny of the village, the harshness of that life in our ancestral world, the boyhood he had been denied.

My father's history of himself exalted rebellion and daring— breaking the law, taking things into one's hands. But it was a different code of conduct that he wanted from his eight sons and daughters. From all of us he wanted order and obedience. The house was to be as quiet as a tomb when he was around. The girls had to stay off balconies. We had to study. Television—by now it had come to Lebanon—was permissible at times. But all, particularly my sisters, had to scurry out of the living room if the scenes in the Egyptian films got particularly steamy and interesting. Life went on in the household when he was away. Then, as soon as the engine of his car was heard, the place became still. He expected the crowd of children to kiss his hand before he left in the

morning and again when he showed up at home in the evening. It was a primitive order broken now and then by capricious excursions into informality and warmth. One child or another would be favored for a day or two; and then, just when that particular son or, on occasion, daughter thought that he had a sure inside track, he was banished—banished without explanation, without cause. The banishment was as arbitrary as the initial favoritism.

I came in for a period of grace. In part it was my grandfather's acceptance of me that recommended me to my father. My interest in what passed for the world of politics and letters was another factor. I was, when my father first turned up in our life, desperate for his attention and approval. I had had so many substitute fathers that I was glad to have the real one around. It was during a brief period of what seemed like harmony between us that my father was told—perhaps by my Aunt Sakiba, or by my grandfather—that I wrote poetry and had published some of it in a couple of obscure student magazines. My father asked for my poetry, and it was duly submitted to him that night. He took the notebook to his bedroom. It was a moment of genuine panic and excitement for me. I expected him to walk out and say a word or two about the poems. But no such luck. The light in his bedroom, which adjoined the "boys' room" was turned off. I waited the next day. But no acknowledgment was to come. The notebooks of poetry just vanished. He said nothing about the poetry he had read, not to me at least.

It came to me indirectly that he found the poems of love and sentiment unbecoming of a young man. By his silence, he had let me know what he thought of the sensibility that created them. Men wrote of the world of politics, of public affairs and history. Men wrote about the eternal crisis of the south of Lebanon, of the waters of the Litani River rushing to the sea, bypassing the

thirsty villages of the south; they wrote about Arab history, about the fight between the Arab and Jew in Palestine. There was no place in this scheme of things for frivolous poems of romance and youth. There was no need to write of love: men bullied women, and women—awed by worldly success, by the aura of a man—just submitted. This was what my father knew, this way of looking at the world had worked for him. It worked for him when Nadia slipped out at dusk and met him in the *trancha*, the underground army shelter, or at the foot of Beaufort. It had worked, too, with Naima, the peasant woman with the white thighs and the full figure, and with Umm Ahmad, the sultry, dark *fellaha*.

Unknown to him while he worked in the Arabian oil fields, or while he sat amidst the intimidated peasants of Arnoun pleading with him for a favor, a new generation of poets was taking the old Arabic language, and the stilted forms of Arabic poetry, and making work more daring, more intimate, blurring the line between prose and poetry, making the latter informal and accessible. In times past, *qasida*, the classical poem, had been the Arabs' favored medium of expression. Stilted, formal, removed from what we knew and experienced—that *qasida*. But a new generation of poets refused to go along and just to submit to the tyranny of the form. They would do what the English Romantic poets did in their time: they would make the poem livelier, freer. And here in our world, where the poet was the chronicler and the lawyer of his tribe, of his community—its defender, the slanderer of its enemies, the extoller of its virtues—the innovators task was more difficult than that of the English Romantics they admired. Poetry was a weapon, a collective possession. New poets were walking away from this entire tradition. A Syrian poet by the name of Nizar Qabbani was my hero: he wrote openly of Beirut's languid evenings, of sexual lust, of the bosom of his beloved, of

what "the brunette" told him. Though I had no great poetic talents, I admired Qabbani's poetry, and, like an admiring schoolboy tracing a drawing he liked, I had copied his style, had done some poor imitations of the great poet, in the poems I submitted to my father. Part of me knew the risk of submitting the poetry to my father. But it was a time when I sought his affection, when I stood in awe of him.

It was hard to make sense of the place of sons and daughters in my father's scheme of things. In the old world into which he was born, children kept the land, cared for the elderly. Children came like the seasons. Life was what it was, and the children were part of what men and women endured and accepted and what they taught themselves to praise. My grandfather's progeny, all ten born to him after the age of forty, was expected to be there for him in his old age—and they were. My grandfather transmitted to his children a whole tradition—with all its sternness and limits. The old man expected the world to hold, and within the limits, to remain a familiar place. In the "new" topsy-turvy world my father was trying to elbow his way through, children were a nuisance and a burden. Masculinity had to be proven by fathering sons. But several sons later, one lost track of the message and the purpose. What remained were claimants to money, to space.

There were fathers in our extended world of kinsmen, in families in transition like our own, who accepted that their time had passed, who knew that our pretentious and changing country required the skills of a younger generation. "Anything for the children," went the saying of such parents. Money was sunk into educating children, and fathers waited to have a second wind through the lives of their sons. My father was a different kind of man, the kind who continued to cruise past the reality of his

limited schooling, who dyed his hair, who continued to think of himself as a "young man" of great promise.

—⁓—

Again from Kafka to his father:

> Care had to be taken so that no scraps fell on the floor. In the end it was under your chair that there were most scraps.

My father wanted pristine ways from his sons and daughters. But wealthy and now divorced, and still comparatively young at not quite forty, my father became one of the out-and-out marauders of our small world. Mistresses came and went. He picked up the more glamorous ones in the modern sector of the city on days when he drove my brothers and me to spend the day at the beaches of Beirut. One favored mistress, Adalat, a woman of striking good looks and grace, was rumored to be a candidate for marriage. She must have been in her early thirties, most likely a young widow. She was around quite a bit and tried to teach my father new ways. In her own quiet and gentle way, she suggested to him to be more open and "modern" with his daughters, to be less strict and tyrannical with his sons. I hoped that the rumors of marriage would come true. But having walked into the bedroom without a wedding, Adalat had forfeited her chance of marriage.

With Adalat—and other mistresses—by his side, with his money and flamboyant renditions of his achievements, my father cut a striking figure in the still drab and small world of our kinsmen. He declared himself one of the "great hopes" of Southern Lebanon. He acquired the services of a man who use to be the

"courtier" of Adel Bey Osseiran, one of the big men of the south. The great political lord had banished him, and he was now stuck with a much lesser man. But without money of his own—only "great skills"—he did his best to polish up my father. The courtier went with my father wherever he went, told him that he was still very young, that so much of his promise lay ahead of him, that a great future in politics awaited him. The courtier was good with words; the years by Adel Bey Osseiran's side had served him well. In 1960, when I was fifteen and my father was forty-one, someone floated the idea that my father should run for the country's parliament in the district of Nabatiyya. It was a year when a cousin of my father's had run for election to a parliamentary seat. We were becoming dreamers of better things to come. The balance of expectations, the order of things was being loosened. But my father knew the odds, and the matter of a political future remained idle talk. He knew that he had been away, he was aware of the education that he didn't have; no fool, he understood he would be fleeced along the way and come out of the venture empty-handed.

The world beyond always tugged at him. He was desperate to make the leap; he took great pride in the fragments of "modernity" he acquired—the car, the bank account, the sunglasses. He developed a passion for neckties. Such were the things that came to him from the new world. But his innate reflexes, the cynicism about men's motives and ideas, or the conviction that the world offered nothing new beyond the chases and the hunts and the duels of men, came from way back, from the village behind us. Once my initial awe of him subsided, it was easy to see the old world clinging to him. He dwelt on my mother's misery, held it up in front of me, tormented me with it. I had assumed that he, the winner, had forgotten, that there was no further need for celebrations of how far he had gone beyond her. But by dwelling

on her fate, on the habits and the bravado and the defects of the Abdullahs as much as he did, it was easy to see that he, like my mother, was in the grip of the past.

A few years earlier, I had stepped beyond my mother's world and had begun to see it as one of the old tales and superstitions. She had offered token resistance and nothing more. In reality, she had welcomed the venture, taken pride in it. My mother's relation to the modern world had been an easy one: she didn't know it, she was indifferent to it. She dealt with the modern world from the security of an established old world of her own. She was on one bank of a river; I was on the other. She understood that I had to make my way through worlds that she herself could neither enter nor master.

Now my father presented a wholly different problem. He was too proud and too brittle and too competitive to hail my passage and that of my brother to something more evolved and less hellish than his world. He could not trust us with interpreting the new order of things, with pursuing dreams of our own. And it was too late for him to change and learn new ways. My father's new money was now sending me to the best American prep school in the city. But from that school I had to return to what I now saw as an embarrassing medieval order from a vanished world. David Miller, a young American teacher, taught "free inquiry" and skepticism, and taught with irreverence; my father asked for submission. The ritual of kissing his hand twice became an act of resented capitulation to a world that ceased to hold me. Around us there were fathers who were dispensing with the ritual, who had begun to understand that our country was no longer its old self, that their children had glimpsed the outline of a different order. But my father, in and out of the country, held onto some

of the old ways. They must have been his props, his way of feeling at home.

The world was opening up to me—nothing grand or fundamental, just small cracks here and there. I was beginning to "see." It was easy to see that my father often tried to carry a political discussion by outshouting the other man, that his grasp of public issues, impressive in a gathering of men with limited education, was strained in more accomplished company. It was very easy to see that my father had never read a book from cover to cover. A friend of my father's from his youth had done one of those things that the folklore of a poor and ambitious population ennobled: he had studied by "kerosene lamp," made his way to the university while working as a government teacher, studied law, and had risen in the judiciary to a respected judgeship. It was easy to see that my father either deferred to him to the point of excessive meekness or tried to dismiss him with a stridency that gave away his own sense of having been betrayed by the world.

It was easy, too, to recognize in my father's methods of control and humiliation old tricks. He found some religious scripture, some old saying that said that perhaps a man may be granted by God the All-Knowing and the All-Seeing his wishes through a daughter without knowing it. My father had resented the power of his sisters; he had complained about the ease with which they had overruled him and outmaneuvered him in his father's domain. Now, with a family of his own, he propped up his oldest daughter, my half-sister, three or four years younger than myself, to taunt his sons. She "was almost a man," he said of her. Perhaps she could be the first Shia woman PhD in the country. My sister was all too willing to oblige. She had a talent, this daughter, for distinguishing the sound of his car's engine from the tumult that came in from the street below. No sooner had she heard the

slamming of his car's door, than she was deep into her books, the dutiful daughter keeping the temptations of the world at bay. Muslim law specified that a daughter inherited only half what a son did. My sister was not the first, nor the last, daughter to spend a lifetime trying to get around this law.

After using his oldest daughter to browbeat his sons, my father was, as always, quick to discard her. He knew that a life of schooling was not for her. But the old methods were the ones he knew. To him came a view of the world as a struggle over limited things. He offered up the same old world.

My father searched for a footing in the country and couldn't find it. Like so many of the country's emigrants who made money in faraway places and who now were beginning to show up with what they accumulated abroad, he could not master the place. The applause given, the money earned spent on sumptuous meals and relatives and children and mistresses, the doors that mattered remained hard to go through. My father sank some money into a construction company and some into a fancy restaurant on one of the beaches of Beirut. The construction company—with the grand name of Orient Associated Contractors—caved under when his partner was arrested on charges of smuggling across the Lebanese-Israeli border. My father was left with the modern office furniture of the company, with its Land Rover—and with the Maltese-born wife of his partner. (My father preferred to say that she was an English woman.) As for the restaurant—Samhu, I think it was called—it stood there jinxed and without customers. The restaurant was just across the road from the crowded beach, the beach where my brothers and I spent many of our summer days. We took pride in my father's restaurant whenever we drove by. It should have been a perfect location for a thriving restaurant. But the place just failed.

—⁓—

From Alexander Mitscherlich's *Society Without the Father*:

> What does one really inherit from one's father, apart from his physique, perhaps, and what does one acquire from him? What happens in emotional communication with him, and what social task is associated with this relationship? One can admire one's father, one can feel sheltered and protected by him, or one can fear him; and finally one can despise him. At different times one can do all these things. Besides these so varying emotional attitudes, however, there is something else. One can learn from one's father, one can be initiated by him into ways of dealing with things, or one can do without him in the process.

I had to do without my father, and I had to get around him. Between us stood an old grievance—my mother's tale of defeat—and the messages and temptations of a new world. He had vanquished my mother. But she, such a vivid artist, her vision sharpened by obsession and defeat, had etched a portrait of him in my mind. And he, after a brief period of promise between us, then walked over and silhouetted himself against the old unflattering portrait. Without much effort, the two merged.

My mother had hated his eyes. Like searchlights, I now saw his eyes—inspecting everyone, doubting everyone. I saw him standing there at the gates of a wider world that I wanted to break into. He claimed that he understood where I wanted to go. At times, when I was willing to obey, when I was able to live up to

his expectations, he said he was ready to help me get there. Then there were times when he fell back on the old saying that he had learned on the land: each man should pull his own thorns with his own hands. Tyranny at times, abdication of any responsibility at others. This was my father.

My father and I possessed completely different temperaments. And hard as I had tried to be what he wanted, hard as the emissaries between us tried to bridge the gap, hard as he himself tried, to the best of his ability, to introduce a touch of liberality and openness into his code, the different temperaments wrote our story.

My father exalted competition. It was what he knew and lived by. Of a man he admired, he said that this one was a real man who "ate the egg and its shell." In other words, the man took his share and the share of others. I could not applaud the man he liked. I did not want to sit at the table of the man who ate the egg and its shell.

VII

◀━━◎◯◎━━▶

Fathers and sons, ancestors and descendants, once stood on common ground. Then the ground cracked. And the crack widened into a chasm that sons (and daughters) filled with alternate displays of concealment and rebellion, and parents with intimidation and terror. King Shahryar in *One Thousand and One Nights* had railed against women: "There is no woman but who cuckolds her husband; may the curse of Allah be upon one and all and upon the fools who lean against them for support and who place the reins of conduct in their hands." Fathers had picked up where King Shahryar had left off. Yet there was springing up in the relations between young men and women in my world a new kind of tenderness and protectiveness. What was a realm of conquest was becoming a realm of shared vulnerability. Young women couldn't see some of the sensitive boys around them—writing poetry but hiding it from their fathers, dodging the sermons of the elders—as hyenas. Young men couldn't see the young women—juggling different centuries in the air, getting beaten for

walking onto the balcony, for using the family telephone—as malicious schemers. Young men and women became fellow sufferers in a world of repression and yearning.

Some, to be sure, did their parents one better and "became" their parents. But so many around me broke out of the net—or tried to.

My own alienation had been deep. My American school had made it all that much worse. Lawrence of Arabia had once said of the American schools in the Arab world—schools brought there by missionaries anxious to bring the Gospel and educate—that these schools "without intention taught revolution." I don't know about revolution. Mine was a different time. Lawrence was speaking of the early American push into the Arab world in the latter part of the nineteenth century, of the explosive mix of "high Oriental atmosphere" and the new American ideas. What I do know is that David Miller, and another engaging teacher by the name of Mr. Eddington, were my first teachers who taught without bullying techniques, the first to give warrant to a measure of independence. They were different men, the two Americans: the older, slightly disheveled Mr. Eddington whose first name we never knew, and the younger, more intense David Miller, with his crew cut and the narrow tie and glasses.

It was David Miller who signaled the unlamented death of the old teaching methods the day he brought an album of Harry Belafonte and a record player to class. The song that made an impression was about John Henry outperforming a steam engine with a hammer. From the entire song, I retained only, "John Henry was a man…." But what remained was the sight of the young American who had come to us. David Miller told tantalizing tales of buying an old "clunker" of a car and driving from coast to coast. It was easy

to see a new beginning in that vast and unencumbered faraway land, to graft onto it all one's youthful dreams.

I owe to David Miller something more tangible than the dream of a youngster traversing a big land in an old clunker: from him I picked up the appreciation of the language of the *Ingliz* and its literature. It was David Miller who assigned *A Tale of Two Cities*. Once I read it, the romance with the language became an affair of the heart. I loved the contrasts in the opening lines: "It was the best of times, it was the worst of times, it was the age of wisdom, it was the age of foolishness, it was the epoch of belief, it was the epoch of incredulity, it was the season of light, it was the season of darkness…." The novel's narrow streets, winding streets "full of offence and stench" were familiar to me. And so was the rain running in "eccentric fits" into houses. That had been the world of my childhood. And so were the "knitting women" by the guillotine: they, too, didn't seem like a creation of a novelist's mind. There were "knitting women" in my world.

I committed to memory—for I read it so many times—the treasured last lines of Sydney Carton as he was about to sacrifice his own life for the woman he loved: "It is a far, far better thing that I do, than I have ever done; it is a far, far better rest that I go to than I have ever known."

I had come to my American school from an environment that differed from that of its usual students. I leaned on the world of my school. The main trail through the small pine forest on the school grounds led to a clearing with a stunning view of the Mediterranean. A tunnel elsewhere on the grounds led to a private rocky beach with a light house. I liked the "assembly," the American teachers, "PE," the joy of my first locker. There was the thrill of learning from Sami Fadlallah, trendy Sami Fadlallah, who was at home in the snack bars of West Beirut, who wore a

faded pair of Levi's with the coveted red label on the back pocket, more prestigious than any new pair of jeans. This bliss, this wonder: we had arrived. It must have been for something like this that we had all fled the land.

So starkly different, the two worlds seemed like night and day. The ancestor's world on one side, the foreigners' world on the other. I split myself between the two. My father's rage, his commands and his reproaches, came in the ancestor's language. There was a time when my father, now working in Liberia, came back with a few words of pidgin English: "Bring wata," "I am businessman from Lebanon." Using the few words in a gathering of unlettered women and relatives, my father's whole edifice of might crumbled in front of me. It was not his world or his language. I played along, indulged his vanity when he threw around those few words of English.

When miserly Hafiza said, "You have a piaster, you are worth a piaster," she said it in Arabic. Rendered it into English, it was comical. Saying it in the original gave it the full might, the full and damning power of a materialistic society that at times seemed oblivious to all other standards of judgments. I who had so few piasters—my father was the one with the piasters—preferred the mocking English version.

It was Arabic, the older language, that was insinuating. The new language seemed so free of innuendo, so direct. It was hard to insinuate in the new language that the woman of virtue was really a whore, that the man winking and telling of his sexual triumphs with other men's sisters and wives was really a cuckold. One wink and one parable of the old language sealed a man's fate, summoned his past, exhumed his dead, took away his mystery. The tentative new language, hiding so little, coming as it did for me out of a social and historical void, answered my need.

—⁘—

The alienation led in one direction: I desperately wanted to get out of the country. The decision—nothing heroic, nothing special about it, typical of so many—came in 1962, when I was seventeen. This was the country's gift to me: the fear of being trapped. But I had to bide my time, petition and plead. There would be no easy exit out of the place. Money was an obstacle. And my family had a way of going sour on you right when you needed it, had a way of insisting how essential was your presence in the country for everyone around you right when you were desperate to break out.

A year after I had caught the bug, my older brother left for America. Our country now had a busy airport, and he had conceived a romantic idea that he—the son and grandson of two women who would not sweep the floor at night for fear of disturbing the spirits—should go out and return with a degree in aircraft engineering. He scoured the catalogues of American colleges, wore out their pages. He could not appreciate the force, the magnitude of this kind of break between generations. But he had made it. I was to wait a decent interval.

Our kinsmen were not turning the new world out there—its degrees and universities—into props of an old world. Things were happening quickly, and with great frenzy, among a people who had no whole world of their own. Fathers with basic reading skills and illiterate mothers now wanted lawyers and physicians and PhDs for sons and sons-in-law. It was said that a young man with an advanced degree fetched a handsome dowry. Woe to the fathers with so many daughters.

The fixed boundaries of our world were as stubborn as ever. The themes of our world were beginning to repeat. Ahmad Bey al Assad, the big boss of the south of Lebanon, had died and had

bequeathed his dominion to his son Kamel Bey al Assad. And it was known that Kamel had a son named Ahmad. It was too easy to guess that the old publisher who owned the two magazines, *The Net* and *The Fisherman*, was going to trap buxom young women and write about the episode in hints and insinuations in his next weekly column. Our world closed in. And when it closed in on young men, when they were unable to get out of the country, they succumbed to migraine headaches, broke down, threatened suicide, grew frenzied and desperate. They knew the same streets; they had sat in on the same conversations. Endless plans were discussed, and none of them ever materialized. There would be repeated trips to the post office in downtown Beirut. The post office boxes would be opened time and again by anxious young men waiting for deliverance.

There was a time—it was the worst of times—when a young man was no longer a boy but had not yet earned the spurs of manhood. This was where I stood in my last two years in the country.

My prop—the school I liked—had gone. I was now attending a Lebanese Muslim school where the chemistry teacher's experiments always ended up with a broken tube and where a teacher allergic to all things American and Western lectured on the evils that Orientalism and Orientalists did to the Muslim world. I did not know or care, nor did anyone else in class, about Orientalism and Orientalists. Mr. Farukh, Omar Farukh, never bothered to explain who the Orientalists were and what they did. For his passions and for his knowledge, Mr. Farukh needed a more appreciative audience. He ranged over Islamic philosophy, Islamic history. But we didn't dare ask about the Orientalists. Someone had told the basher of Orientalists and the enemies of Islam that I had come to his school from an American school. His sermons about cowboy culture—pronounced *coy-boy*—always ended in a

query: "Don't you think so, Ajami?" Yes, Mr. Farukh, it is indeed so; it is always so and will always be so.

The most glamored young man in the extended clan was Munir, the son of Najib Bey Alawiyya. Munir was a generation older than us, a smuggler. The line of work he was in gave him an aura of danger, of a man braving the rules, doing what he wanted. It was a strange transformation: Munir was his parents' only child, born to them when they were both old and had given up hope of having children. He had grown up, protected and pampered, in a silent and still house in a Christian suburb; gendarmes had always escorted him to school. He, the dutiful son, had gone on to study law at a Jesuit university, Saint Joseph University, before then going on to an envied career in the Customs Department. It was in that world, in a port city of trade and smuggling, that Munir had been seduced. The easy money, the women—the temptation had been too great. Munir had slipped into the orbit of a famed smuggler, one Sami al-Khuri. The thin and intense Sami al-Khuri, one of the great traffickers of the region, had made his fortune and his name smuggling cigarettes to Tangier and drugs to Europe and the United States. He was a man of great glamor: he wore silk suits; he had a gigantic black deaf-mute for a bodyguard and a beach house north of the city where he kept an assortment of beautiful foreign women from Greece and Italy and France and Malta, the flotsam of the Mediterranean.

The life Munir led—the sports cars he drove around the city, the money he was so easy and generous with to the Greek woman who bore him a child out of wedlock—put him way beyond the life of our large clan. We, his younger cousins, could only dream of such fulfillment. Then calamity struck. Sami al-Khuri and Munir disappeared, never to be heard from again. They had run afoul, it was known in the way such things were known, of a

more powerful smuggler in Jordan, a member of the royal family. Rumor had it that the two of them had been killed and buried in the desert wilderness, somewhere in Jordan. The disappearance of the two men became one of the great stories of the city. Hucksters and impostors of every kind promised the grief-stricken parents of Munir that they knew where their son was, that, for the right price, they could spring him out of captivity. Fortunetellers made their way to the quiet house in the suburbs where Munir's parents lived. The retired colonel and his wife had only known a life of order and success and command. Now, near the end, in old age, their world had come apart. They had not been used to sorrow, the old couple.

The life of my family—the larger circle of kinsmen—seemed to make less and less sense. The further we tried to get away from the land and the past, the more unsettled we seemed to get. Rival households within the same clan fought over things that were not theirs to fight over: seats in Parliament, Cabinet posts, large clinics and small hospitals for the sons who were going to be great physicians.

The river made its way to the sea. The houses of stone—white, hard stone—took years to complete. And when they rose, they bore no relation to the ambitious blueprints. The pressure on the children became even more intense. The dreams—yesterday made up of soothing chatter shared by everyone in the household, making possible flights from harsh realities—had to be redeemed, made good on or abandoned. The dream of marrying off a daughter, giving her a grand wedding and a dowry worth the honor of her family and the quality of the young man she was marrying, clashed with the dream of educating her brothers. A circle was closed: in the rural world, my father and uncles and aunts, and my peers' fathers and uncles and aunts, had been in the way of one

another. A quarter-century later, the themes repeated. Only there were more of us. Our fathers, circumcised, had been potent; our women had been fertile. No wonder our Maronite countrymen had insisted on keeping the head of the Census Bureau their own preserve: our country rested on the old prop that the Christians were the majority. Only the swelling number of Muslims was disturbing the balance of this fragile place. The Census Bureau could look away, but trouble loomed over the horizon.

—◊—

The fulfilled dreams of two young men from the town of Nabatiyya came to my rescue. Both had gone off to America and returned with a title the *Franji* world awarded: a PhD in Political Science. The degree glamored the two of them—and, by extension, their entire clan—in the small world being awakened to new pretensions and possibilities.

Both men were elected to Parliament; both rose to Cabinet appointments. One of the two was a man with fair skin, slightly effeminate ways, and a manner so finicky that one got the impression that he viewed the world out there as a nuisance. But he was admired for this finicky manner. Such was the reason why degrees were obtained. One had to be able to snub other men. He was named Minister of Planning.

The second was a sensitive and substantial man. But his tale ended in sorrow. He married for money and was promised a great fortune by his father-in-law, a dowry worthy of his degree, worthy of his Cabinet post. But the father-in-law had not come up with what he had promised. And then tragedy struck: at the height of his fame—and exposure—the bright man with an American education died of a heart attack.

The great tale of the two men with American degrees had unfolded a few kilometers away from our village. Their tale was one easily assimilated in our clan: the new world could be made to serve and exalt an old one. Ministers in the Cabinet paved the hard roads to the

tucked-away villages, brought licenses for more tobacco acreage, avenged old slights, settled old accounts, even comforted the dead. There would be a huge dowry for the brave. A decision was made that I should go to America and get a PhD in Political Science.

At the time, my father was away working in Libya. I set out with my grandfather's blessing for the passage. He was the one who secured the sum from the loan shark that made possible my departure. Two dreams were rolled into one: the old world's dream of honor and status, and my desperate need to get away.

—ᴨᴨ—

The ancestors were their imperturbable selves. They had been through such things before. They had seen the comings and goings of their descendants. Of this passage they said: "We have bequeathed this one young man, as we have bequeathed so many others like him, a restricted world. Our descendants will carry the restrictions within them. We have marked out borders in their minds. Beyond these borders they are unable to go. In a faraway place, this descendant with a foreign education will squirm, refuse to get into the same elevator with the neighbor's dog. This descendant's grandmother never approached prayer when one of the pariah dogs in the village, one of the dogs with protruding ribs, came close to her. The dog 'defiled' her. This descendant squirming about sharing the elevator with a dog may rename

the aversion to dogs and call it an 'allergy.' But the border and the prohibitions will hold.

"We have sworn our descendants to a code of silence. We taught them, on pain of banishment and dishonor, to leave things, so many things, unnamed. The gift of our world—the gift of discretion, of leaving things unnamed or renaming them, of leaving undisturbed nooks and crannies and hidden terrors—has been imparted to this descendant. So much of what this descendant has seen will be consigned to some hidden vault that will be left unlocked to gather the dust. He may want to scream, this descendant. He will be tempted to play with words; his mother's curse, a lifetime of words, floods and hurricanes of words, may have seeped into him. He may want to tell of what he has seen; he may want to remove that decent veil of obscurity. Even this one—taunted every now and then about being 'his mother's son'—will not dare transgress those sacred limits. Beyond those limits, he knows, there is the *wa'ar*, the heath, where hyenas run, where dark solitude is the fate of those banished from the folk. There are forbidden zones, zones of *ayb*, shame and honor: these are vast impenetrable realms. We know this one, he will never go there with a searchlight, he will never escort strangers and guide them into these zones. We have always had our *hakawatis*, storytellers, who in days past, in those fabled Arab cities of memory that slipped through the fingers, sat down in coffeehouses to tell benign enchanting stories at dusk. Behind the shutters, in those hidden vaults, there were stories that would have put the best *hakawatis* to shame.

"We have no apologies to offer this descendant: none are needed. We gave, we withheld, we were hard on him in the same way the elders were hard on us. We gave this descendant what was there to be given. The small things given—like the walks the boy

took with his grandfather, or the slingshot made for the boy by his grandfather's shepherd, or the first pair of long pants bought by an aunt for a boy anxious for long pants—will be made grand with the passage of time. Everyone here was denied. Nature denied our birthplace. Our landscape was harsh. Our olive trees didn't give. Hard as the trees were shaken, furious as a mother-in-law got with her son's wife who had gathered the olives, there still wasn't enough olive oil for a year's supply. Mightier powers than ourselves disposed of our fate; and this, too, will become clear with the passage of time in the eyes of a descendant wanting to judge. A young man with *asl*, with roots, with good blood, will understand that the mighty father who thundered at home was thwarted in government bureaus where he was always a stranger and a petitioner. He will understand that the grandfather who kept aloof from the world did so because there were bigger men than he in the world beyond the small village. We tormented. But such were our ways, passed on to us, passed on to him.

> "Oblivion will take care of a good deal of the hurt. It is hard to summon pain. But our blood flows in every descendant's veins, and they will all understand."

—ᴡᴡ—

Prior to his departure for America, Fouad, the grandson of Shaykh Muhammad, was taken by his grandfather to his great-grandfather's grave in Arnoun's dusty cemetery, just a few yards beyond the houses of the village, past cactus and tangled brush and stones. (We bury our ancestors close by; they watch and we remember.) The traveler was told to "return a man." Life

in *ghurba*, in the land of strangers, was belittled and mocked on that day; the land and its ways and the clan were exalted.

We release our young men, send them away. But we count on their oblivion and understanding. Above all, we count on their silence. They are not to breach the code; they are to make their journey seem like the normal comings and goings of a family known for its ventures to distant lands.

There is a Muslim appeal to God: *Ya Sattar*, "Thou who veilest." All things are to be left unsaid, covered. That attribute of God is as important as His mercy or compassion or power or all-encompassing knowledge. The veiling was to be honored by all—those who stayed and those who packed up and left.

The country—the land and the ancestors—visited men in faraway places in dreams. From the dreams, they woke up terrified. And, then, they walked out into the light. In the presence of strangers they paid homage to the country, told its tales, said how good it had been to them, how hard it had been to leave its shores. They remembered its cool running streams and the swish of its pine needles and the fragrance of its orange blossoms and the echoes of church bells in its valleys. As was predicted by the ancestors, the spare, hard country was made grand by the passage of time. The descendants crossed into the world of strangers with the phobias of those ancestors with whom they were fated to remain in an intimate animosity.

No one was quite sure where Montevideo lay, but the grizzled man leading his grandson to the cemetery had gone there, fathered children, and had returned to this remote, forlorn village in southern Lebanon. Migration was in the blood: the grave the young traveler was led to was the burial place of a man who had come from Persia—another country with fury and a spell—in the middle years of the nineteenth century. Still, the land was to

be extolled, and the young traveler was to make the voyage seem like the confident deed of someone who could have chosen to stay on the land, in the certitude of his world and the protection of his clan.

Formal passport shot of Fouad

Fouad's mother

I could not indulge the country's tales of itself or honor—as fully expected of everyone born to my culture—my people's code of silence. I loved my birthplace—and I pitied it. My love, it took for granted. It assumed that all its children were under its spell. It believed what outsiders said of its charm and beauty. It had the testimonies of so many men of means, of eloquence. It did not have to deign to acknowledge my love. Perhaps it knew that my love for it was only fidelity to childhood—to those fragments of our lives that we yearn for and fear.

As for pity, the place was too vain for pity. To understand the pity of others, a place, a people, has to look within itself; it has to have a sense of incompleteness to come to terms with its disorder. That, the country was unable to do. You can pity vanity. But vanity has no way of understanding pity. Besides, as the country saw things, I had no standing that entitled me to pity it. As a stepchild without means, without great claims, my pity could always be taken as despair and bitterness.

In quitting Lebanon I closed a circle. A century and ten years after my great-grandfather had adopted the country, I was the first of his progeny to leave with no intention of ever returning. For me, the spell was broken. I was able to find within me Dahir the Persian's ability to undertake a passage without return. Devouring fragments of Persian history in the 1850s, picking up the footsteps of travelers who went through the place during Dahir's time, reading the dispassionate reports of diplomats deciphering the ways of Dahir's land, I think of him bidding farewell to his country. Remembering my mother stitching into my pocket her offering of the American dollars she was able to scrape together, I think of him, of Dahir, departing with a few coins from the place that was home: a place he must have loved and that he must have been anxious to flee.

I was not to see Lebanon again until 1974—a decade after my departure. I was traveling to an academic conference in India to practice my trade. It was one of my first such trips, perhaps my very first. I had not known the stops until I had boarded the plane. It was a serene, sunny day in midwinter. The landscape that came into view as the plane began its descent—the mountains cascading to the sea, the land dotted with slopes of vineyards, the white buildings shimmering in the sun, and above us the clear light—looked imposing and sane, the kind of landscape

that would ensnare the unknowing, the kind that someone with a return ticket and a settled world to sustain them could fall for. Druze and Maronite, Sunni and Shia, Abu Fawzi and his privileged half-brother who got away with most of the inheritance because he was the son of the favored wife, the young boy and his terrifying father whom he loathed, the sinister woman spinning damaging yarns and one of her victims who for so long lived under a cloud—they could all be taken in together, and from this altitude, they could all share this place.

But I knew that I could not come here for the sights and the climate and the ruins. I knew that for me this could not be a country like any other. The recurrence of my dream about being trapped in the country that I experienced during the very long hour I spent in the transit lounge, the terror that I might be stranded here again, was more than enough to compensate for the guilt that I had passed through the place without even a nod in the direction of my family. I stuck close to the other travelers going through the place. And the great tumult of arrival in India, in a place that held for me no memories, seemed tame after the brief encounter with the ghosts.

I was to return on two short visits in the years to come. But the place no longer held me; it was no longer home. From a distance, I could do what had to be done for my mother. She had yearned for a place of her own; now I could provide it. She had insisted back in those years of toil and disinheritance—when she lived in the shadow of her failure and divorce—that there would be vindication at the end of the road. What I had done with life was enough to offer that vindication. Beyond that, I could not go: my family's world remained riddled with a tangle of a hundred little scores to settle. I could not be part of their feuds.

I visited my uncle Abbas in Monrovia in the summer of 1977. In part, the journey was made to honor the man who, back when I needed kindness and protection, was there for me. In part, I was driven out of curiosity to see those fabled lands of West Africa that had been part of our imagination. Monrovia—a squalid port city—was a terrible disappointment. The pillared mansions of the Americo-Liberian elite and their Masonic Temple and Baptist churches—the attempts of this elite at a parody of America—were overwhelmed by the filth of the place. To see Monrovia with its muddy and unpaved streets, its seedy bars and night clubs and the prostitutes on the sidewalks was to come face to face with our despair. We had situated our dreams in places of terrible bleakness.

Three years after I had made this visit, the edifice that the Americo-Liberian elites built, the world into which my family had come would be brought to an end. In a land where power had been the preserve of the settlers who had come from America and their descendants, a young man from the country, an outcast, Master Sergeant Samuel Kanyon Doe, and his band of hungry soldiers seized power, killed, and disemboweled the president. Ten days after the coup, thirteen men, the best of the old elite, were paraded nearly naked through the streets of Monrovia, taken to the seashore, tied to seaside posts, and executed. The event had been staged for the television cameras. A vast crowd was at hand to celebrate this deed of vengeance. My uncle's fortunes, a battery factory and a bottling cap business with shiny new machines he was so proud to own, had been tied to men of the old regime. In 1960, as a boy of fourteen, I had gone to a printer in the city of Beirut and had printed more than a thousand glossy calendars with the picture of Liberia's president, William Tubman, and had them shipped to my uncle in Monrovia. It was a small token of his loyalty to the old chief. I had loved the assignment; I had taken

some pride in the printing job, in the words I had chosen to put under Tubman's picture. "President William Tubman: Prosperity and Progress." It was Tubman's immediate successor, William Tolbert, an ordained Baptist minister, who had been gunned down and disemboweled by the rebels, the young men from the countryside. The bottling cap business and the battery factory were abandoned by my uncle.

But my uncle knew no other world, had no other skills. He could not return to Lebanon. By then, Lebanon itself was deep into its long season of ruin. He set out for Guinea for yet another try in Africa. By the time he was felled by cancer at age sixty, Abbas had circled the continent. It had given him what was there to be gotten in countries of such great distress. He had, like others, sleepwalked through those foreign places. Lebanon held them. They returned from God's remote places with whatever they accumulated to be blessed and to be accepted by the land. For me, the spell was broken.

It was easier to think of Abbas as I had known him before his passage. In his youth he had been a hunter with a sleek Saluki named Laika that had been his steady companion in the village. He had loved the solitude of his parents' rock-strewn vineyard at the foot of Beaufort Castle; it was there that he put together a thatched hut on stilts where he spent his summer nights. On the same spot where the hut had stood, he had built, with the money from Africa, a large house of white stone, away from the village and a short walk from the rocks that overlooked the Litani River and the plains below and the paved road that coiled like a black snake to my mother's town in the valley. The house, with its back to the vineyard and a wide front porch that overlooked the village, had taken years to complete. It had been built in installments, whenever there was money to add to it. Breaking away

from the village was Abbas's special gift: in the time and place, it was the mark of an independent temperament. It bespoke a man who knew city ways, who had been awakened to new stirrings, who had an aesthetic judgment of his own. It was in that half-built house that Abbas's wedding had been celebrated when he came to marry in the old country. He had married into one of the great feudal families of the south. Much had happened. The search for a bride had been the ambition of his sisters, rooted in the anxiety about the family's place in the pecking order. My aunts had been thorough. There had been feuds within the family over the "piece of land" on which the house was built, anger from Abbas's older brothers, who believed that the land granted their younger brother by my grandparents was proof that he had been favored by their parents. The three other brothers had asked for equal treatment, for land of their own. But larger claims would write the story of this house.

In the early 1980s I would see the house of Abbas's dreams in the television footage. I would see it in the background, a house of white stone on a rocky hill, soldiers in jeeps and tanks going by, helicopters circling overhead. Young men with assault rifles, Palestinian gunmen—strangers, *gharibs*, as the Arnounis would have put it—staked their claim to the village. From the tumbled ramparts of Beaufort they could see the old land their parents and elders had quit when they took to the road some three decades earlier. On a clear day the boys with guns and pamphlets, and no apologies to offer men and women whose lives they overturned with such sudden power and fury, swore they could glimpse the hills and fields of Galilee and the road back to a lost paradise. The walls of Acre beckoned them from afar. Then other strangers followed. Beaufort was exalted now: the old neglected fortress, it was said, had become "strategic." It would be shelled and demolished

in the vicious cycle of raids and reprisals between the Israelis and the Palestinians. History—larger feuds than my family's—had visited that house in the vineyard.

But I owned a special knowledge of what had gone into this house; I knew its older and more private and, for me, more gripping history. It was there, on that ridge by the castle, where my mother had gone when the grief of her life, and the ways of this somber village, overwhelmed her. Like the boys who would see Galilee from the ramparts, she would see the threshing fields and the spring and the water wheels of her youth in her town in the valley. It was there, on cool summer nights in Abbas's house, where the descendants of the man from Tabriz said how much they loved the land and the sacred earth and the immemorial ways as they scrambled to find a way out of its grip.

My grandfather, my anchor in the old country, had died two or three years before all of this—when his small world was still his own, before the Time of Troubles and the grand "events" that shattered the cocoon of his village and the country beyond. In a world of so many masks and disguises, the old landholder, who once might have strolled uphill from his house in the center of the village to his vineyard at the foot of Beaufort to inspect the masons at work on his son's house, would have been a stranger. Cruelty came in large doses.

A grand funeral was given him. A vast crowd of his countless descendants came to Arnoun to bid him farewell. There was a dangerous curve on the road between Arnoun and Nabatiyya, a curve that the authorities had always promised to straighten out and repair and had always neglected to do so. The authorities of Nabatiyya did the needed work on it in anticipation of the funeral crowd that would come to Arnoun. The shaykh was useful in his death as he had been in his life, it was said of him. Surly

peasants, Arnounis who had come of age, who had declared their rebellion against the age-old subservience of their class, who had stayed away from the funerals of my grandmother's brothers, were there in droves. A new world—a new world storming in with a vengeance that the Arnounis feared as they had always feared the unknown—loomed over the horizon, over the old slights and limits they knew. The landholder they laid to rest in the summer of 1973 was their link to an irretrievable past.

He was buried right alongside his father in a green mausoleum with dripped paint and iron railings, not far from his house, in the back of the village, at the end of a dusty and parched trail on the other side of the villa of my grandmother's parents. Their graves were held in a gray, lancet-shaped mausoleum that stood at the entrance of Arnoun. The mausoleum had more stone and iron—and more symmetry—than all the hovels of the Arnounis.

Acknowledgments

In a small graveyard in the countryside, dotted with American flags on Memorial Day for the veterans who reach back to the Revolutionary War, Fouad's marker stands out. It's not only the foreignness of his name that distinguishes it, but the addition of one other—the only addition he insisted on—the name of his ancestral village where he was born: Arnoun. The juxtaposition captures everything he was. For all his academic training, for all his intense book learning and studious observation of the world around him—political and social—the core of his being, the root of all his responses, the base of his wisdom were in the lessons that came out of that village. Like Melville's whaling ship, it was his Harvard and Yale. And his deep love of America came down to the values its people fought and died for. The America he encountered in Lebanon was, in many ways, the best of itself—individuals who believed that all people, everywhere desire and deserve the rights and freedoms and dignity we have always aspired to. All his life, he held a firm belief in the importance of America's role in the world. In these fundamental ways, this autobiography goes to the essence of who he was.

In early 2020, I visited Leon Wieseltier at the D.C. offices of his new publication. He was in the first stages of launching

Liberties and asked, almost immediately, if there was anything unpublished by Fouad that he could include in the magazine. When I told him about an autobiography of some hundreds of handwritten pages, he gave me three months to get it typed. The debt I owe him not only for this encouragement but for his great enthusiasm on reading it is more than I can put into words. The version that has come to print is the work of a very talented young writer and editor, Benjamin Kravitz, who spent countless hours sifting out repetitions and detours that took the reader too far from the story. His graceful touch with the text and the voice of the author was essential. Marty Peretz was an early reader, as were Sheila and Afshin Molavi. Their emotional responses were a reflection of its fidelity to a man they loved. Elizabeth Kaplan took on this endeavor with genuine excitement, and the poise and professionalism she brought to our effort was all the assurance I needed. Heather King has been a joy to work with—a copy editor with a light and intelligent red pen. Megan Ring has been there through everything, as she was for Fouad. Peter Theroux's consent to write a foreword was a joyful surprise. He does us—Fouad and me—great honor. To Adam Bellow go my deepest thanks—for his spontaneous embrace of this manuscript, his belief in its worth as a document for all time—a message in a bottle, as he put it—and his patient shepherding of the whole process to bring this to light.